A MODEST PROPOSAL
&
Other Short Satires

First Warbler Classics Edition 2025

"A Modest Proposal" published in 1729 | "The Battle of the Books" published in 1704 | "The Episode of Bentley and Wotton" published in 1704 | "A Meditation Upon a Broomstick" published in 1710 | "Predictions for the Year 1708" published in 1708 | "An Argument Against Abolishing Christianity" published in 1708 | "A Discourse Concerning the Mechanical Operation of the Spirit" published in 1710 | "Hints Towards an Essay on Conversation" published around 1762

Biographical Timeline © 2025 Warbler Press

warblerpress.com

ISBN 978-1-965684-62-7 (paperback)
ISBN 978-1-965684-63-4 (ebook)

A MODEST PROPOSAL
&
Other Short Satires

JONATHAN SWIFT

warbler classics

CONTENTS

A Modest Proposal

*For preventing the children of poor people in Ireland,
from being a burden on their parents or country,
and for making them beneficial to the publick.*

I T IS A melancholy object to those, who walk through this great town, or travel in the country, when they see the streets, the roads, and cabbin-doors crowded with beggars of the female sex, followed by three, four, or six children, all in rags, and importuning every passenger for an alms. These mothers, instead of being able to work for their honest livelihood, are forced to employ all their time in stroling to beg sustenance for their helpless infants who, as they grow up, either turn thieves for want of work, or leave their dear native country, to fight for the Pretender in Spain, or sell themselves to the Barbadoes.

I think it is agreed by all parties, that this prodigious number of children in the arms, or on the backs, or at the heels of their mothers, and frequently of their fathers, is in the present deplorable state of the kingdom, a very great additional grievance; and therefore whoever could find out a fair, cheap and easy method of making these children sound and useful members of the commonwealth, would deserve so well of the publick, as to have his statue set up for a preserver of the nation.

But my intention is very far from being confined to provide only for the children of professed beggars: it is of a much greater extent, and shall take in the whole number of infants at a certain age, who are born of parents in effect as little able to support them, as those who demand our charity in the streets.

As to my own part, having turned my thoughts for many years upon this important subject, and maturely weighed the several schemes of our projectors, I have always found them grossly mistaken in their computation. It is true, a child just dropt from its dam, may be supported by her milk, for a solar year, with little other nourishment: at most not above the value of two shillings, which the mother may certainly get, or the value in scraps, by her lawful occupation of begging; and it is exactly at one year old that I propose to provide for them in such a manner, as, instead of being a charge upon their parents, or the parish, or wanting food and raiment for the rest of their lives, they shall, on the contrary, contribute to the feeding, and partly to the clothing of many thousands.

There is likewise another great advantage in my scheme, that it will prevent those voluntary abortions, and that horrid practice of women murdering their bastard children, alas! too frequent among us, sacrificing the poor innocent babes, I doubt, more to avoid the expence than the shame, which would move tears and pity in the most savage and inhuman breast.

The number of souls in this kingdom being usually reckoned one million and a half, of these I calculate there may be about two hundred thousand couple, whose wives are breeders; from which number I subtract thirty thousand couple, who are able to maintain their own children, (although I apprehend there cannot be so many under the present distresses of the kingdom) but this being granted, there will remain a hundred and seventy thousand breeders. I again subtract fifty thousand, for those women who miscarry, or whose children die by accident or disease within the year. There only remain a hundred and twenty thousand children of poor parents annually born. The question therefore is, How this number shall be reared and provided for? which, as I have already said, under the present situation of affairs, is utterly impossible by all the methods hith-erto proposed. For we can neither employ them in handicraft or agriculture; they neither build houses, (I mean in the country) nor cultivate land: they can very seldom pick up a livelihood by stealing till they arrive at six years old; except where they are of towardly parts, although I confess they learn the rudiments much earlier; during which time they can however be properly looked upon only as probationers; as I have been informed by a principal gentleman in the county of Cavan, who protested to me, that he never knew above one or two instances under the age of six, even in a part of the kingdom so renowned for the quickest proficiency in that art.

I am assured by our merchants, that a boy or a girl, before twelve years old, is no saleable commodity, and even when they come to this age, they will not yield above three pounds, or three pounds and half a crown at most, on the exchange; which cannot turn to account either to the parents or kingdom, the charge of nutriments and rags having been at least four times that value.

I shall now therefore humbly propose my own thoughts, which I hope will not be liable to the least objection.

I have been assured by a very knowing American of my acquaintance in London, that a young healthy child well nursed, is, at a year old, a most delicious nourishing and wholesome food, whether stewed, roasted, baked, or boiled; and I make no doubt that it will equally serve in a fricasee, or a ragoust.

I do therefore humbly offer it to publick consideration, that of the hundred and twenty thousand children, already computed, twenty thousand may be reserved for breed, whereof only one fourth part to be males; which is more than we allow to sheep, black cattle, or swine, and my reason is, that these children are seldom the fruits of marriage, a circumstance not much regarded by our savages, therefore, one male will be sufficient to serve four females. That the remaining hundred thousand may, at a year old, be offered in sale to the persons of quality and fortune, through the kingdom, always advising the mother to let them suck plentifully in the last month, so as to render them plump, and fat for a good table. A child will make two dishes at an entertainment for friends, and when the family dines alone, the fore or hind quarter will make a reasonable dish, and seasoned with a little pepper or salt, will be very good boiled on the fourth day, especially in winter.

I have reckoned upon a medium, that a child just born will weigh 12 pounds, and in a solar year, if tolerably nursed, encreaseth to 28 pounds.

I grant this food will be somewhat dear, and therefore very proper for landlords, who, as they have already devoured most of the parents, seem to have the best title to the children.

Infant's flesh will be in season throughout the year, but more plentiful in March, and a little before and after; for we are told by a grave author, an eminent French physician, that fish being a prolifick dyet, there are more children born in Roman Catholick countries about nine months after Lent, than at any other season; therefore, reckoning a year after Lent, the markets will be more glutted than usual, because the number of Popish infants, is at least three to one in this kingdom, and therefore it will have one other collateral advantage, by lessening the number of Papists among us.

I have already computed the charge of nursing a beggar's child (in which list I reckon all cottagers, labourers, and four-fifths of the farmers) to be about two shillings per annum, rags included; and I believe no gentleman would repine to give ten shillings for the carcass of a good fat child, which, as I have said, will make four dishes of excellent nutritive meat, when he hath only some particular friend, or his own family to dine with him. Thus the squire will learn to be a good landlord, and grow popular among his tenants, the mother will have eight shillings neat profit, and be fit for work till she produces another child.

Those who are more thrifty (as I must confess the times require) may flay the carcass; the skin of which, artificially dressed, will make admirable gloves for ladies, and summer boots for fine gentlemen.

As to our City of Dublin, shambles may be appointed for this purpose, in the most convenient parts of it, and butchers we may be assured will not be wanting; although I rather recommend buying the children alive, and dressing them hot from the knife, as we do roasting pigs.

A very worthy person, a true lover of his country, and whose virtues I highly esteem, was lately pleased in discoursing on this matter, to offer a refinement upon my scheme. He said, that many gentlemen of this kingdom, having of late destroyed their deer, he conceived that the want of venison might be well supplied by the bodies of young lads and maidens, not exceeding fourteen years of age, nor under twelve; so great a number of both sexes in every county being now ready to starve for want of work and service: and these to be disposed of by their parents if alive, or otherwise by their nearest relations. But with due deference to so excellent a friend, and so deserving a patriot, I cannot be altogether in his sentiments; for as to the males, my American acquaintance assured me from frequent experience, that their flesh was generally tough and lean, like that of our schoolboys, by continual exercise, and their taste disagreeable, and to fatten them would not answer the charge. Then as to the females, it would, I think, with humble submission, be a loss to the publick, because they soon would become breeders themselves: and besides, it is not improbable that some scrupulous people might be apt to censure such a practice, (although indeed very unjustly) as a little bordering upon cruelty, which, I confess, hath always been with me the strongest objection against any project, how well soever intended.

But in order to justify my friend, he confessed, that this expedient was put into his head by the famous Psalmanaazor, a native of the island Formosa, who came from thence to London, above twenty years ago, and in conversation told my friend, that in his country, when any young person happened to be put to death, the executioner sold the carcass to persons of quality, as a prime dainty; and that, in his time, the body of a plump girl of fifteen, who was crucified for an attempt to poison the Emperor, was sold to his imperial majesty's prime minister of state, and other great mandarins of the court in joints from the gibbet, at four hundred crowns. Neither indeed can I deny, that if the same use were made of several plump young girls in this town, who without one single groat to their fortunes, cannot stir abroad without a chair, and appear at a playhouse and assemblies in foreign fineries which they never will pay for, the kingdom would not be the worse.

Some persons of a desponding spirit are in great concern about that vast number of poor people, who are aged, diseased, or maimed; and I have been desired to employ my thoughts what course may be taken, to ease the nation of so grievous an incumbrance. But I am not in the least pain upon that matter, because it is very well known, that they are every day dying, and rotting, by cold and famine, and filth, and vermin, as fast as can be reasonably expected. And as to the young labourers, they are now in almost as hopeful a condition. They cannot get work, and consequently pine away from want of nourishment, to a degree, that if at any time they are accidentally hired to common labour, they have not strength to perform it, and thus the country and themselves are happily delivered from the evils to come.

I have too long digressed, and therefore shall return to

my subject. I think the advantages by the proposal which I have made are obvious and many, as well as of the highest importance.

For first, as I have already observed, it would greatly lessen the number of Papists, with whom we are yearly overrun, being the principal breeders of the nation, as well as our most dangerous enemies, and who stay at home on purpose with a design to deliver the kingdom to the Pretender, hoping to take their advantage by the absence of so many good Protestants, who have chosen rather to leave their country, than stay at home and pay tithes against their conscience to an episcopal curate.

Secondly, The poorer tenants will have something valuable of their own, which by law may be made liable to a distress, and help to pay their landlord's rent, their corn and cattle being already seized, and money a thing unknown.

Thirdly, Whereas the maintainance of a hundred thousand children, from two years old, and upwards, cannot be computed at less than ten shillings a piece per annum, the nation's stock will be thereby encreased fifty thousand pounds per annum, besides the profit of a new dish, introduced to the tables of all gentlemen of fortune in the kingdom, who have any refinement in taste. And the money will circulate among our selves, the goods being entirely of our own growth and manufacture.

Fourthly, The constant breeders, besides the gain of eight shillings sterling per annum by the sale of their children, will be rid of the charge of maintaining them after the first year.

Fifthly, This food would likewise bring great custom to taverns, where the vintners will certainly be so prudent as to procure the best receipts for dressing it to perfection; and consequently have their houses frequented by all the fine gentlemen, who justly value themselves upon their knowledge in good eating; and a skilful cook, who understands how to oblige his guests, will contrive to make it as expensive as they please.

Sixthly, This would be a great inducement to marriage, which all wise nations have either encouraged by rewards, or enforced by laws and penalties. It would encrease the care and tenderness of mothers towards their children, when they were sure of a settlement for life to the poor babes, provided in some sort by the publick, to their annual profit instead of expence. We should soon see an honest emulation among the married women, which of them could bring the fattest child to the market. Men would become as fond of their wives, during the time of their pregnancy, as they are now of their mares in foal, their cows in calf, or sows when they are ready to farrow; nor offer to beat or kick them (as is too frequent a practice) for fear of a miscarriage.

Many other advantages might be enumerated. For instance, the addition of some thousand carcasses in our exportation of barrel'd beef: the propagation of swine's flesh, and improvement in the art of making good bacon, so much wanted among us by the great destruction of pigs, too frequent at our tables; which are no way comparable in taste or magnificence to a well grown, fat yearling child, which roasted whole will make a considerable figure at a Lord Mayor's feast, or any other publick entertainment. But this, and many others, I omit, being studious of brevity.

Supposing that one thousand families in this city, would be constant customers for infants flesh, besides others who might have it at merry meetings, particularly at weddings and christenings, I compute that Dublin would take off annually about twenty thousand carcasses; and the rest of the kingdom (where probably they will be sold somewhat cheaper) the remaining eighty thousand.

I can think of no one objection, that will possibly be raised against this proposal, unless it should be urged, that the number of people will be thereby much lessened in the kingdom. This

I freely own, and was indeed one principal design in offering it to the world. I desire the reader will observe, that I calculate my remedy for this one individual Kingdom of Ireland, and for no other that ever was, is, or, I think, ever can be upon Earth. Therefore let no man talk to me of other expedients: Of taxing our absentees at five shillings a pound: Of using neither clothes, nor houshold furniture, except what is of our own growth and manufacture: Of utterly rejecting the materials and instruments that promote foreign luxury: Of curing the expensiveness of pride, vanity, idleness, and gaming in our women: Of introducing a vein of parsimony, prudence and temperance: Of learning to love our country, wherein we differ even from Laplanders, and the inhabitants of Topinamboo: Of quitting our animosities and factions, nor acting any longer like the Jews, who were murdering one another at the very moment their city was taken: Of being a little cautious not to sell our country and consciences for nothing: Of teaching landlords to have at least one degree of mercy towards their tenants. Lastly, of putting a spirit of honesty, industry, and skill into our shopkeepers, who, if a resolution could now be taken to buy only our native goods, would immediately unite to cheat and exact upon us in the price, the measure, and the goodness, nor could ever yet be brought to make one fair proposal of just dealing, though often and earnestly invited to it.

Therefore I repeat, let no man talk to me of these and the like expedients, till he hath at least some glympse of hope, that there will ever be some hearty and sincere attempt to put them into practice.

But, as to myself, having been wearied out for many years with offering vain, idle, visionary thoughts, and at length utterly despairing of success, I fortunately fell upon this proposal, which, as it is wholly new, so it hath something solid and real, of no expence and little trouble, full in our own power, and whereby we can incur no danger in disobliging England. For this kind of commodity will not bear exportation, and flesh being of too tender a consistence, to admit a long continuance in salt, although perhaps I could name a country, which would be glad to eat up our whole nation without it.

After all, I am not so violently bent upon my own opinion, as to reject any offer, proposed by wise men, which shall be found equally innocent, cheap, easy, and effectual. But before something of that kind shall be advanced in contradiction to my scheme, and offering a better, I desire the author or authors will be pleased maturely to consider two points. First, As things now stand, how they will be able to find food and raiment for a hundred thousand useless mouths and backs. And secondly, There being a round million of creatures in humane figure throughout this kingdom, whose whole subsistence put into a common stock, would leave them in debt two million of pounds sterling, adding those who are beggars by profession, to the bulk of farmers, cottagers and labourers, with their wives and children, who are beggars in effect; I desire those politicians who dislike my overture, and may perhaps be so bold to attempt an answer, that they will first ask the parents of these mortals, whether they would not at this day think it a great happiness to have been sold for food at a year old, in the manner I prescribe, and thereby have avoided such a perpetual scene of misfortunes, as they have since gone through, by the oppression of landlords, the impossibility of paying rent without money or trade, the want of common sustenance, with neither house nor clothes to cover them from the inclemencies of the weather, and the most inevitable prospect of intailing the like, or greater miseries, upon their breed for ever.

I profess in the sincerity of my heart, that I have not the least personal interest in endeavouring to promote this necessary work, having no other motive than the publick good of my country, by advancing our trade, providing for infants, relieving the poor, and giving some pleasure to the rich. I have no children, by which I can propose to get a single penny; the youngest being nine years old, and my wife past child-bearing.

The Battle of the Books

A Full and True Account of the Battle Fought Last Friday Between the Ancient and the Modern Books in Saint James's Library.

THE BOOKSELLER TO THE READER

THIS DISCOURSE, AS it is unquestionably of the same author, so it seems to have been written about the same time, with "The Tale of a Tub;" I mean the year 1697, when the famous dispute was on foot about ancient and modern learning. The controversy took its rise from an essay of Sir William Temple's upon that subject; which was answered by W. Wotton, B.D., with an appendix by Dr. Bentley, endeavouring to destroy the credit of Æsop and Phalaris for authors, whom Sir William Temple had, in the essay before mentioned, highly commended. In that appendix the doctor falls hard upon a new edition of Phalaris, put out by the Honourable Charles Boyle, now Earl of Orrery, to which Mr. Boyle replied at large with great learning and wit; and the Doctor voluminously rejoined. In this dispute the town highly resented to see a person of Sir William Temple's character and merits roughly used by the two reverend gentlemen aforesaid, and without any manner of provocation. At length, there appearing no end of the quarrel, our author tells us that the BOOKS in St. James's Library, looking upon themselves as parties principally concerned, took up the controversy, and came to a decisive battle; but the manuscript, by the injury of fortune or weather, being in several places imperfect, we cannot learn to which side the victory fell.

I must warn the reader to beware of applying to persons what is here meant only of books, in the most literal sense. So, when Virgil is mentioned, we are not to understand the person of a famous poet called by that name; but only certain sheets of paper bound up in leather, containing in print the works of the said poet: and so of the rest.

THE PREFACE OF THE AUTHOR

SATIRE IS A sort of glass wherein beholders do generally discover everybody's face but their own; which is the chief reason for that kind reception it meets with in the world, and that so very few are offended with it. But, if it should happen otherwise, the danger is not great; and I have learned from long experience never to apprehend mischief from those understandings I have been able to provoke: for anger and fury, though they add strength to the sinews of the body, yet are found to relax those of the mind, and to render all its efforts feeble and impotent.

There is a brain that will endure but one scumming; let the owner gather it with discretion, and manage his little stock with husbandry; but, of all things, let him beware of bringing it under the lash of his betters, because that will make it all bubble up into impertinence, and he will find no new supply. Wit without knowledge being a sort of cream, which gathers in a night to the top, and by a skilful hand may be soon whipped into froth; but once scummed away, what appears underneath will be fit for nothing but to be thrown to the hogs.

A Full and True Account of the Battle Fought Last Friday Between the Ancient and the Modern Books in Saint James's Library.

WHOEVER EXAMINES, WITH due circumspection, into the nnual records of time,[1] will find it remarked that War is the child of Pride, and Pride the daughter of Riches:—the former of which assertions may be soon granted, but one cannot so easily subscribe to the latter; for Pride is nearly related to Beggary and Want, either by father or mother, and sometimes by both: and, to speak naturally, it very seldom happens among men to fall out when all have enough; invasions usually travelling from north to south, that is to say, from poverty to plenty. The most ancient and natural grounds of quarrels are lust and avarice; which, though we may allow to be brethren, or collateral branches of pride, are certainly the issues of want. For, to speak in the phrase of writers upon politics, we may observe in the republic of dogs, which in its original seems to be an institution of the many, that the whole state is ever in the profoundest peace after a full meal; and that civil broils arise among them when it happens for one great bone to be seized on by some leading dog, who either divides it among the few, and then it falls to an oligarchy, or keeps it to himself, and then it runs up to a tyranny. The same reasoning also holds place among them in those dissensions we behold upon a turgescency in any of their females. For the right of possession lying in common (it being impossible to establish a property in so delicate a case), jealousies

---

1   Riches produeeth pride ; Pride is war's ground, &c., Vid. Ephem. de *Mary Clarke;* opt. Edit.

and suspicions do so abound, that the whole commonwealth of that street is reduced to a manifest state of war, of every citizen against every citizen, till some one of more courage, conduct, or fortune than the rest seizes and enjoys the prize: upon which naturally arises plenty of heart-burning, and envy, and snarling against the happy dog. Again, if we look upon any of these republics engaged in a foreign war, either of invasion or defence, we shall find the same reasoning will serve as to the grounds and occasions of each; and that poverty or want, in some degree or other (whether real or in opinion, which makes no alteration in the case), has a great share, as well as pride, on the part of the aggressor.

Now whoever will please to take this scheme, and either reduce or adapt it to an intellectual state or commonwealth of learning, will soon discover the first ground of disagreement between the two great parties at this time in arms, and may form just conclusions upon the merits of either cause. But the issue or events of this war are not so easy to conjecture at; for the present quarrel is so inflamed by the warm heads of either faction, and the pretensions *somewhere or other* so exorbitant, as not to admit the least overtures of accommodation. This quarrel first began, as I have heard it affirmed by an old dweller in the neighbourhood, about a small spot of ground, lying and being upon one of the two tops of the hill Parnassus; the highest and largest of which had, it seems, been time out of mind in quiet possession of certain tenants, called the Ancients; and the other was held by the Moderns. But these disliking their present station, sent certain ambassadors to the Ancients, complaining of a great nuisance; how the height of that part of Parnassus quite spoiled the prospect of theirs, especially towards the east; and therefore, to avoid a war, offered them the choice of this alternative, either that the Ancients would please to remove themselves and their effects down to the lower summit, which the Moderns would graciously surrender to them, and advance into their place; or else the said Ancients will give leave to the Moderns to come with shovels and mattocks, and level the said hill as low as they shall think it convenient. To which the Ancients made answer, how little they expected such a message as this from a colony whom they had admitted, out of their own free grace, to so near a neighbourhood. That, as to their own seat, they were aborigines of it, and therefore to talk with them of a removal or surrender was a language they did not understand. That if the height of the hill on their side shortened the prospect of the Moderns, it was a disadvantage they could not help; but desired them to consider whether that injury (if it be any) were not largely recompensed by the shade and shelter it afforded them. That as to the levelling or digging down, it was either folly or ignorance to propose it if they did or did not know how that side of the hill was an entire rock, which would break their tools and hearts, without any damage to itself. That they would therefore advise the Moderns rather to raise their own side of the hill than dream of pulling down that of the Ancients; to the former of which they would not only give licence, but also largely contribute. All this was rejected by the Moderns with much indignation, who still insisted upon one of the two expedients; and so this difference broke out into a long and obstinate war, maintained on the one part by resolution, and by the courage of certain leaders and allies; but, on the other, by the greatness of their number, upon all defeats affording continual recruits. In this quarrel whole rivulets of ink have been exhausted, and the virulence of both parties enormously augmented. Now, it must be here understood, that ink is the great missive weapon in all battles of the learned, which, conveyed through a sort of engine called a *quill*, infinite numbers of these are darted at the enemy by the valiant on each side, with equal skill and violence, as if it were an engagement of porcupines. This malignant liquor was compounded, by the engineer who invented it, of two ingredients, which are, gall and copperas; by its bitterness and venom to suit, in some degree, as well as to foment, the genius of the combatants. And as the Grecians, after an engagement, when they could not agree about the victory, were wont to set up trophies on both sides, the beaten party being content to be at the same expense, to keep itself in countenance (a laudable and ancient custom, happily revived of late in the art of war), so the learned, after a sharp and bloody dispute, do, on both sides, hang out their trophies too, whichever comes by the worst. These trophies have largely inscribed on them the merits of the cause; a full impartial account of such a Battle, and how the victory fell clearly to the party that set them up. They are known to the world under several names; as disputes, arguments, rejoinders, brief considerations, answers, replies, remarks, reflections, objections, confutations. For a very few days they are fixed up all in public places, either by themselves or their representatives,[2] for passengers to gaze at; whence the chiefest and largest are removed to certain magazines they call *libraries*, there to remain in a quarter purposely assigned them, and thenceforth begin to be called *Books of Controversy*.

In these books is wonderfully instilled and preserved the spirit of each warrior while he is alive; and after his death his soul transmigrates thither to inform them. This, at least, is the more common opinion; but I believe it is with libraries as with other cemeteries, where some philosophers affirm that a certain spirit, which they call *brutum hominis*, hovers over the monument, till the body is corrupted and turns to dust or to worms, but then vanishes or dissolves; so, we may say, a restless spirit haunts over every book, till dust or worms have seized upon it—which to some may happen in a few days, but to others later—and

---

2   Their title pages.

therefore, books of controversy being, of all others, haunted by the most disorderly spirits, have always been confined in a separate lodge from the rest, and for fear of a mutual violence against each other, it was thought prudent by our ancestors to bind them to the peace with strong iron chains. Of which invention the original occasion was this: When the works of Scotus first came out, they were carried to a certain library, and had lodgings appointed them; but this author was no sooner settled than he went to visit his master Aristotle, and there both concerted together to seize Plato by main force, and turn him out from his ancient station among the divines, where he had peaceably dwelt near eight hundred years. The attempt succeeded, and the two usurpers have reigned ever since in his stead; but, to maintain quiet for the future, it was decreed that all polemics of the larger size should be hold fast with a chain.

By this expedient, the public peace of libraries might certainly have been preserved if a new species of controversial books had not arisen of late years, instinct with a more malignant spirit, from the war above mentioned between the learned about the higher summit of Parnassus.

When these books were first admitted into the public libraries, I remember to have said, upon occasion, to several persons concerned, how I was sure they would create broils wherever they came, unless a world of care were taken; and therefore I advised that the champions of each side should be coupled together, or otherwise mixed, that, like the blending of contrary poisons, their malignity might be employed among themselves. And it seems I was neither an ill prophet nor an ill counsellor; for it was nothing else but the neglect of this caution which gave occasion to the terrible fight that happened on Friday last between the Ancient and Modern Books in the King's library. Now, because the talk of this battle is so fresh in everybody's mouth, and the expectation of the town so great to be informed in the particulars, I, being possessed of all qualifications requisite in an historian, and retained by neither party, have resolved to comply with the urgent importunity of my friends, by writing down a full impartial account thereof.

The guardian of the regal library—a person of great valour—but chiefly renowned for his *humanity*, had been a fierce champion for the Moderns, and, in an engagement upon Parnassus, had vowed with his own hands to knock down two of the ancient chiefs who guarded a small pass on the superior rock, but, endeavouring to climb up, was cruelly obstructed by his own unhappy weight and tendency towards his centre, a quality to which those of the Modern party are extremely subject; for, being light-headed, they have, in speculation, a wonderful agility, and conceive nothing too high for them to mount, but, in reducing to practice, discover a mighty pressure about their posteriors and their heels. Having thus failed in his design, the disappointed champion bore a cruel rancour to the Ancients, which he resolved to gratify by showing all marks of his favour to the books of their adversaries, and lodging them in the fairest apartments; when, at the same time, whatever book had the boldness to own itself for an advocate of the Ancients was buried alive in some obscure corner, and threatened, upon the least displeasure, to be turned out of doors. Besides, it so happened that about this time there was a strange confusion of place among all the books in the library, for which several reasons were assigned. Some imputed it to a great heap of learned dust, which a perverse wind blew off from a shelf of Moderns into the keeper's eyes. Others affirmed he had a humour to pick the worms out of the schoolmen, and swallow them fresh and fasting, whereof some fell upon his spleen, and some climbed up into his head, to the great perturbation of both. And lastly, others maintained that, by walking much in the dark about the library, he had quite lost the situation of it out of his head; and therefore, in replacing his books, he was apt to mistake and clap Descartes next to Aristotle, poor Plato had got between Hobbes and the *Seven Wise Masters,* and Virgil was hemmed in with Dryden on one side and Wither on the other.

Meanwhile, those books that were advocates for the Moderns, chose out one from among them to make a progress through the whole library, examine the number and strength of their party, and concert their affairs. This messenger performed all things very industriously, and brought back with him a list of their forces, in all, fifty thousand, consisting chiefly of light-horse, heavy-armed foot, and mercenaries; whereof the foot were in general but sorrily armed and worse clad; their horses large, but extremely out of case and heart; however, some few, by trading among the Ancients, had furnished themselves tolerably enough.

While things were in this ferment, discord grew extremely high; hot words passed on both sides, and ill blood was plentifully bred. Here a solitary Ancient, squeezed up among a whole shelf of Moderns, offered fairly to dispute the case, and to prove by manifest reason that the priority was due to them from long possession, and in regard of their prudence, antiquity, and, above all, their great merits toward the Moderns. But these denied the premises, and seemed very much to wonder how the Ancients could pretend to insist upon their antiquity, when it was so plain (if they went to that) that the Moderns were much the more ancient[3] of the two. As for any obligations they owed to the Ancients, they renounced them all. "It is true," said they, "we are informed some few of our party have been so mean as to borrow their subsistence from you, but the rest, infinitely the greater number (and especially we French and English), were so far from stooping to so base an example, that there never passed, till this very hour, six words between us. For our horses were of

---

3 According to the modern paradox.

our own breeding, our arms of our own forging, and our clothes of our own cutting out and sewing." Plato was by chance up on the next shelf, and observing those that spoke to be in the ragged plight mentioned a while ago, their jades lean and foundered, their weapons of rotten wood, their armour rusty, and nothing but rags underneath, he laughed loud, and in his pleasant way swore, by G——, he believed them!

Now, the Moderns had not proceeded in their late negotiation with secrecy enough to escape the notice of the enemy. For those advocates who had begun the quarrel, by setting first on foot the dispute of precedency, talked so loud of coming to a battle, that Sir William Temple happened to overhear them, and gave immediate intelligence to the Ancients, who thereupon drew up their scattered troops together, resolving to act upon the defensive; upon which, several of the Moderns fled over to their party, and among the rest Temple himself. This Temple, having been educated and long conversed among the Ancients, was, of all the Moderns, their greatest favourite, and became their greatest champion.

Things were at this crisis when a material accident fell out. For upon the highest corner of a large window, there dwelt a certain spider, swollen up to the first magnitude by the destruction of infinite numbers of flies, whose spoils lay scattered before the gates of his palace, like human bones before the cave of some giant. The avenues to his castle were guarded with turnpikes and palisadoes, all after the modern way of fortification. After you had passed several courts you came to the centre, wherein you might behold the constable himself in his own lodgings, which had windows fronting to each avenue, and ports to sally out upon all occasions of prey or defence. In this mansion he had for some time dwelt in peace and plenty, without danger to his person by swallows from above, or to his palace by brooms from below; when it was the pleasure of fortune to conduct thither a wandering bee, to whose curiosity a broken pane in the glass had discovered itself, and in he went, where, expatiating a while, he at last happened to alight upon one of the outward walls of the spider's citadel; which, yielding to the unequal weight, sunk down to the very foundation. Thrice he endeavoured to force his passage, and thrice the centre shook. The spider within, feeling the terrible convulsion, supposed at first that nature was approaching to her final dissolution, or else that Beelzebub, with all his legions, was come to revenge the death of many thousands of his subjects whom his enemy had slain and devoured. However, he at length valiantly resolved to issue forth and meet his fate. Meanwhile the bee had acquitted himself of his toils, and, posted securely at some distance, was employed in cleansing his wings, and disengaging them from the ragged remnants of the cobweb. By this time the spider was adventured out, when, beholding the chasms, the ruins, and dilapidations of his fortress, he was very near at his wit's end; he stormed and swore like a madman, and swelled till he was ready to burst. At length, casting his eye upon the bee, and wisely gathering causes from events (for they know each other by sight), "A plague split you," said he; "is it you, with a vengeance, that have made this litter here; could not you look before you, and be d—n'd? Do you think I have nothing else to do (in the devil's name) but to mend and repair after you?" "Good words, friend," said the bee, having now pruned himself, and being disposed to droll; "I'll give you my hand and word to come near your kennel no more; I was never in such a confounded pickle since I was born." "Sirrah," replied the spider, "if it were not for breaking an old custom in our family, never to stir abroad against an enemy, I should come and teach you better manners." "I pray have patience," said the bee, "or you'll spend your substance, and, for aught I see, you may stand in need of it all, towards the repair of your house." "Rogue, rogue," replied the spider, "yet methinks you should have more respect to a person whom all the world allows to be so much your betters." "By my troth," said the bee, "the comparison will amount to a very good jest, and you will do me a favour to let me know the reasons that all the world is pleased to use in so hopeful a dispute." At this the spider, having swelled himself into the size and posture of a disputant, began his argument in the true spirit of controversy, with resolution to be heartily scurrilous and angry, to urge on his own reasons without the least regard to the answers or objections of his opposite, and fully predetermined in his mind against all conviction.

"Not to disparage myself," said he, "by the comparison with such a rascal, what art thou but a vagabond without house or home, without stock or inheritance? born to no possession of your own, but a pair of wings and a drone-pipe. Your livelihood is a universal plunder upon nature; a freebooter over fields and gardens; and, for the sake of stealing, will rob a nettle as easily as a violet. Whereas I am a domestic animal, furnished with a native stock within myself. This large castle (to show my improvements in the mathematics) is all built with my own hands, and the materials extracted altogether out of my own person."

"I am glad," answered the bee, "to hear you grant at least that I am come honestly by my wings and my voice; for then, it seems, I am obliged to Heaven alone for my flights and my music; and Providence would never have bestowed on me two such gifts without designing them for the noblest ends. I visit, indeed, all the flowers and blossoms of the field and garden, but whatever I collect thence enriches myself without the least injury to their beauty, their smell, or their taste. Now, for you and your skill in architecture and other mathematics, I have little to say: in that building of yours there might, for aught I know, have been labour and method enough; but, by woeful experience for us both, it is too plain the materials are naught; and I hope you will henceforth take warning, and consider duration and matter, as well as method and art. You boast, indeed, of being obliged to no other creature, but of drawing and spinning out all from yourself; that is to say, if we may judge of the liquor in the vessel by what issues out, you possess a good plentiful store of dirt and poison in your breast; and, though I would by no means lesson or disparage your genuine stock of either, yet I doubt you are somewhat obliged, for an increase of both, to a little foreign assistance. Your inherent portion of dirt does not fall of acquisitions, by sweepings exhaled from below; and one insect furnishes you with a share of poison to destroy another. So that, in short, the question comes all to this: whether is the nobler being of the two—that which, by a lazy contemplation of four inches round, by an overweening pride, feeding, and engendering on itself, turns all into excrement and venom, producing nothing at all but flybane and a cobweb; or that which, by a universal range, with long search, much study, true judgment, and distinction of things, brings home honey and wax?"

This dispute was managed with such eagerness, clamour, and warmth, that the two parties of books, in arms below, stood silent a while, waiting in suspense what would be the issue; which was not long undetermined: for the bee, grown impatient at so much loss of time, fled straight away to a bed of roses, without looking for a reply, and left the spider, like an orator, collected in himself, and just prepared to burst out.

It happened upon this emergency that Æsop broke silence first. He had been of late most barbarously treated by a strange effect of the regent's *humanity*, who had torn off his title-page, sorely defaced one half of his leaves, and chained him fast among a shelf of Moderns. Where, soon discovering how high the quarrel was likely to proceed, he tried all his arts, and turned himself to a thousand forms. At length, in the borrowed shape of an ass, the regent mistook him for a Modern; by which means he had time and opportunity to escape to the Ancients, just when the spider and the bee were entering into their contest; to which he gave his attention with a world of pleasure, and, when it was ended, swore in the loudest key that in all his life he had never known two cases, so parallel and adapt to each other as that in the window and this upon the shelves. "The disputants," said he, "have admirably managed the dispute between them, have taken in the full strength of all that is to be said on both sides, and exhausted the substance of every argument *pro* and *con*. It is but to adjust the reasonings of both to the present quarrel, then to compare and apply the labours and fruits of each, as the bee has learnedly deduced them, and we shall find the conclusion fall plain and close upon the Moderns and us. For pray, gentlemen, was ever anything so modern as the spider in his air, his turns, and his paradoxes? he argues in the behalf of you, his brethren, and himself, with many boastings of his native stock and great genius; that he spins and spits wholly from himself, and scorns to own any obligation or assistance from without. Then he displays to you his great skill in architecture and improvement in the mathematics. To all this the bee, as an advocate retained by us, the Ancients, thinks fit to answer, that, if one may judge of the great genius or inventions of the Moderns by what they have produced, you will hardly have countenance to bear you out in boasting of either. Erect your schemes with as much method and skill as you please; yet, if the materials be nothing but dirt, spun out of your own entrails (the guts of modern brains), the edifice will conclude at last in a cobweb; the duration of which, like that of other spiders' webs, may be imputed to their being forgotten, or neglected, or hid in a corner. For anything else of genuine that the Moderns may pretend to, I cannot recollect; unless it be a large vein of wrangling and satire, much of a nature and substance with the spiders' poison; which, however they pretend to spit wholly out of themselves, is improved by the same arts, by feeding upon the insects and vermin of the age. As for us, the Ancients, we are content with the bee, to pretend to nothing of our own beyond our wings and our voice: that is to say, our flights and our language. For the rest, whatever we have got has been by infinite labour and search, and ranging through every corner of nature; the difference is, that, instead of dirt and poison, we have rather chosen to till our hives with honey and wax; thus furnishing mankind with the two noblest of things, which are sweetness and light."

'Tis wonderful to conceive the tumult arisen among the books upon the close of this long descant of Æsop: both parties took the hint, and heightened their animosities so on a sudden, that they resolved it should come to a battle. Immediately the two main bodies withdrew, under their several ensigns, to the farther parts of the library, and there entered into cabals and consults upon the present emergency. The Moderns were in very warm debates upon the choice of their leaders; and nothing less than the fear impending from their enemies could have kept them from mutinies upon this occasion. The difference was greatest among the horse, where every private trooper pretended to the chief command, from Tasso and Milton to Dryden and Wither. The light-horse were commanded by Cowley and Despreaux. There came the bowmen under their valiant leaders, Descartes, Gassendi, and Hobbes; whose strength was such that they could shoot their arrows beyond the atmosphere, never to fall down again, but turn, like that of Evander, into meteors; or, like the cannon-ball, into stars. Paracelsus brought a squadron of stink-pot-flingers from the snowy mountains of Rhætia. There came a vast body of dragoons, of different nations, under the leading of Harvey, their great aga: part armed with scythes, the weapons of death; part with lances and long knives, all steeped in poison; part shot bullets of a most malignant nature, and used white powder, which infallibly killed without report. There came several bodies of heavy-armed foot, all mercenaries, under the ensigns of Guicciardini, Davila, Polydore Vergil, Buchanan, Mariana, Camden, and others. The engineers were commanded by Regiomontanus and Wilkins. The rest was a confused multitude, led by Scotus, Aquinas, and Bellarmine; of mighty bulk and stature, but without either arms, courage, or discipline. In the last place came infinite swarms of *calones*, a disorderly rout led by L'Estrange; rogues and ragamuffins, that follow the camp for nothing but the plunder, all without coats to cover them.

The army of the Ancients was much fewer in number; Homer led the horse, and Pindar the light-horse; Euclid was chief engineer; Plato and Aristotle commanded the bowmen; Herodotus and Livy the foot; Hippocrates, the dragoons; the allies, led by Vossius and Temple, brought up the rear.

All things violently tending to a decisive battle, Fame, who much frequented, and had a large apartment formerly assigned her in the regal library, fled up straight to Jupiter, to whom she delivered a faithful account of all that passed between the two parties below; for among the gods she always tells truth. Jove, in great concern, convokes a council in the Milky Way. The senate assembled, he declares the occasion of convening them; a bloody battle just impendent between two mighty armies of ancient and modern creatures, called *books*, wherein the celestial interest was but too deeply concerned. Momus, the patron of the Moderns, made an excellent speech in their favour, which was answered by Pallas, the protectress of the Ancients. The assembly was divided in their affections; when Jupiter commanded the Book of Fate to be laid before him. Immediately were brought by Mercury three large volumes in folio, containing memoirs of all things past, present, and to come. The clasps were of silver double gilt, the covers of celestial turkey leather, and the paper such as here on earth might pass almost for vellum. Jupiter, having silently read the decree, would communicate the import to none, but presently shut up the book.

Without the doors of this assembly there attended a vast number of light, nimble gods, menial servants to Jupiter: those are his ministering instruments in all affairs below. They travel in a caravan, more or less together, and are fastened to each other like a link of galley-slaves, by a light chain, which passes from them to Jupiter's great toe: and yet, in receiving or delivering a message, they may never approach above the lowest step of his throne, where he and they whisper to each other through a large hollow trunk. These deities are called by mortal men *accidents* or *events;* but the gods call them *second causes.* Jupiter having delivered his message to a certain number of these divinities, they flew immediately down to the pinnacle of the regal library, and consulting a few minutes, entered unseen, and disposed the parties according to their orders.

Meanwhile Momus, fearing the worst, and calling to mind an ancient prophecy which bore no very good face to his children the Moderns, bent his flight to the region of a malignant deity called Criticism. She dwelt on the top of a snowy mountain in Nova Zembla; there Momus found her extended in her den, upon the spoils of numberless volumes, half devoured. At her right hand sat Ignorance, her father and husband, blind with age; at her left, Pride, her mother, dressing her up in the scraps of paper herself had torn. There was Opinion, her sister, light of foot, hood-winked, and head-strong, yet giddy and perpetually turning. About her played her children, Noise and Impudence, Dulness and Vanity, Positiveness, Pedantry, and Ill-manners. The goddess herself had claws like a cat; her head, and ears, and voice resembled those of an ass; her teeth fallen out before, her eyes turned inward, as if she looked only upon herself; her diet was the overflowing of her own gall; her spleen was so large as to stand prominent, like a dug of the first rate; nor wanted excrescences in form of teats, at which a crew of ugly monsters were greedily sucking; and, what is wonderful to conceive, the bulk of spleen increased faster than the sucking could diminish it. "Goddess," said Momus, "can you sit idly here while our devout worshippers, the Moderns, are this minute entering into a cruel battle, and perhaps now lying under the swords of their enemies? who then hereafter will ever sacrifice or build altars to our divinities? Haste, therefore, to the British Isle, and, if possible, prevent their destruction; while I make factions among the gods, and gain them over to our party."

Momus, having thus delivered himself, stayed not for an answer, but left the goddess to her own resentment. Up she rose in a rage, and, as it is the form on such occasions, began a soliloquy: "It is I" (said she) "who give wisdom to infants and idiots; by me children grow wiser than their parents, by me beaux become politicians, and schoolboys judges of philosophy; by me sophisters debate and conclude upon the depths of knowledge; and coffee-house wits, instinct by me, can correct an author's style, and display his minutest errors, without understanding a syllable of his matter or his language; by me striplings spend their judgment, as they do their estate, before it comes into their hands. It is I who have deposed wit and knowledge from their empire over poetry, and advanced myself in their stead. And shall a few upstart Ancients dare to oppose me? But come, my aged parent, and you, my children dear, and thou, my beauteous sister; let us ascend my chariot, and haste to assist our devout Moderns, who are now sacrificing to us a hecatomb, as I perceive by that grateful smell which from thence reaches my nostrils."

The goddess and her train, having mounted the chariot, which was drawn by tame geese, flew over infinite regions, shedding her influence in due places, till at length she arrived at her beloved island of Britain; but in hovering over its metropolis, what blessings did she not let fall upon her seminaries of Gresham and Covent-garden! And now she reached the fatal plain of St. James's library, at what time the two armies were upon the point to engage; where, entering with all her caravan unseen, and landing upon a case of shelves, now desert, but once inhabited by a colony of virtuosos, she stayed awhile to observe the posture of both armies.

But here the tender cares of a mother began to fill her thoughts and move in her breast: for at the head of a troup of Modern bowmen she cast her eyes upon her son Wotton, to whom the fates had assigned a very short thread. Wotton, a young hero, whom an unknown father of mortal race begot by stolen embraces with this goddess. He was the darling of his mother above all her children, and she resolved to go and comfort him. But first, according to the good old custom of deities, she cast about to change her shape, for fear the divinity of her counte-nance might dazzle his mortal sight and overcharge the rest of his senses. She therefore gathered up her person into an octavo compass: her body grow white and arid, and split in pieces with dryness; the thick turned into pasteboard, and the thin into paper; upon which her parents and children artfully strewed a black juice, or decoction of gall and soot, in form of letters: her head, and voice, and spleen, kept their primitive form; and that which before was a cover of skin did still continue so. In this guise she marched on towards the Moderns, indistinguishable in shape and dress from the divine Bentley, Wotton's dearest friend. "Brave Wotton," said the goddess, "why do our troops stand idle here, to spend their present vigour and opportunity of the day? away, let us haste to the generals, and advise to give the onset immediately." Having spoke thus, she took the ugliest of her monsters, full glutted from her spleen, and flung it invisibly into his mouth, which, flying straight up into his head, squeezed out his eye-balls, gave him a distorted look, and half-overturned his brain. Then she privately ordered two of her beloved chil-dren, Dulness and Ill-manners, closely to attend his person in all encounters. Having thus accoutred him, she vanished in a mist, and the hero perceived it was the goddess his mother.

The destined hour of fate being now arrived, the fight began; whereof, before I dare adventure to make a particular description, I must, after the example of other authors, petition for a hundred tongues, and mouths, and hands, and pens, which would all be too little to perform so immense a work. Say, goddess, that presidest over history, who it was that first advanced in the field of battle! Paracelsus, at the head of his dragoons, observing Galen in the adverse wing, darted his javelin with a mighty force, which the brave Ancient received upon his shield, the point breaking in the second fold…(*Hic pauca desunt*)…They bore the wounded aga on their shields to his chariot…(*Desunt nonnulla*)….

Then Aristotle, observing Bacon advance with a furious mien, drew his bow to the head, and let fly his arrow, which missed the valiant Modern and went whizzing over his head; but Descartes it hit; the steel point quickly found a defect in his head-piece; it pierced the leather and the pasteboard, and went in at his right eye. The torture of the pain whirled the valiant bow-man round till death, like a star of superior influence, drew him into his own vortex.

…..(*Ingens hiatus hic in MS.*)….when Homer appeared at the head of the cavalry, mounted on a furious horse, with difficulty managed by the rider himself, but which no other mortal durst approach; he rode among the enemy's ranks, and bore down all before him. Say, goddess, whom he slew first and whom he slew last! First, Gondibert advanced against him, clad in heavy armour and mounted on a staid sober gelding, not so famed for his speed as his docility in kneeling whenever his rider would mount or alight. He had made a vow to Pallas that he would never leave the field till he had spoiled Homer of his armour: madman, who had never once seen the wearer, nor understood his strength! Him Homer overthrew, horse and man, to the ground, there to be trampled and choked in the dirt. Then with a long spear he slew Denham, a stout Modern, who from his father's side derived his lineage from Apollo, but his mother was of mortal race. He fell, and bit the earth. The celestial part Apollo took, and made it a star; but the terrestrial lay wallowing upon the ground. Then Homer slew Sam Wesley with a kick of his horse's heel; he took Perrault by mighty force out of his saddle, then hurled him at Fontenelle, with the same blow dashing out both their brains.

On the left wing of the horse Virgil appeared, in shining armour, completely fitted to his body; he was mounted on a dapple-grey steed, the slowness of whose pace was an effect of the highest mettle and vigour. He cast his eye on the adverse wing, with a desire to find an object worthy of his valour, when behold upon a sorrel gelding of a monstrous size appeared a foe, issuing from among the thickest of the enemy's squadrons; but his speed was less than his noise; for his horse, old and lean, spent the dregs of his strength in a high trot, which, though it made slow advances, yet caused a loud clashing of his armour, terrible to hear. The two cavaliers had now approached within the throw of a lance, when the stranger desired a parley, and, lifting up the visor of his helmet, a face hardly appeared from within which, after a pause, was known for that of the renowned Dryden. The brave Ancient suddenly started, as one possessed with surprise and disappointment together; for the helmet was nine times too large for the head, which appeared situate far in the hinder part, even like the lady in a lobster, or like a mouse under a canopy of state, or like a shrivelled beau from within the penthouse of a modern periwig; and the voice was suited to the visage, sounding weak and remote. Dryden, in a long harangue, soothed up the good Ancient; called him father, and, by a large deduction of genealogies, made it plainly appear that they were nearly related. Then he humbly proposed an exchange of armour, as a lasting mark of hospitality between them. Virgil consented (for the goddess Diffidence came unseen, and cast a mist before his eyes), though his was of gold and cost a hundred beeves, the other's but of rusty iron. However, this glittering armour became the Modern yet worsen than his own. Then they agreed to exchange horses; but, when it came to the trial, Dryden was afraid and utterly unable to mount.

...(*Alter hiatus in MS.*)...Lucan appeared upon a fiery horse of admirable shape, but headstrong, bearing the rider where he list over the field; he made a mighty slaughter among the enemy's horse; which destruction to stop, Blackmore, a famous Modern (but one of the mercenaries), strenuously opposed himself, and darted his javelin with a strong hand, which, falling short of its mark, struck deep in the earth. Then Lucan threw a lance; but Æsculapius came unseen and turned off the point. "Brave Modern," said Lucan, "I perceive some god protects you, for never did my arm so deceive me before: but what mortal can contend with a god? Therefore, let us fight no longer, but present gifts to each other." Lucan then bestowed on the Modern a pair of spurs, and Blackmore gave Lucan a bridle....(*Pauca desunt....*) Creech: but the goddess Dulness took a cloud, formed into the shape of Horace, armed and mounted, and placed in a flying posture before him. Glad was the cavalier to begin a combat with a flying foe, and pursued the image, threatening aloud; till at last it led him to the peaceful bower of his father, Ogleby, by whom he was disarmed and assigned to his repose.

Then Pindar slew——, and—— and Oldham, and——, and Afra the Amazon, light of foot; never advancing in a direct line, but wheeling with incredible agility and force, he made a terrible slaughter among the enemy's light-horse. Him when Cowley observed, his generous heart burnt within him, and he advanced against the fierce Ancient, imitating his address, his pace, and career, as well as the vigour of his horse and his own skill would allow. When the two cavaliers had approached within the length of three javelins, first Cowley threw a lance, which missed Pindar, and, passing into the enemy's ranks, fell ineffectual to the ground. Then Pindar darted a javelin so large and weighty, that scarce a dozen Cavaliers, as cavaliers are in our degenerate days, could raise it from the ground; yet he threw it with ease, and it went, by an unerring hand, singing through the air; nor could the Modern have avoided present death if he had not luckily opposed the shield that had been given him by Venus. And now both heroes drew their swords; but the Modern was so aghast and disordered that he knew not where he was; his shield dropped from his hands; thrice he fled, and thrice he could not escape. At last he turned, and lifting up his hand in the posture of a suppliant, "Godlike Pindar," said he, "spare my life, and possess my horse, with these arms, beside the ransom which my friends will give when they hear I am alive and your prisoner." "Dog!" said Pindar, "let your ransom stay with your friends; but your carcase shall be left for the fowls of the air and the beasts of the field." With that he raised his sword, and, with a mighty stroke, cleft the wretched Modern in twain, the sword pursuing the blow; and one half lay panting on the ground, to be trod in pieces by the horses' feet; the other half was borne by the frighted steed through the field. This Venus took, washed it seven times in ambrosia, then struck it thrice with a sprig of amaranth; upon which the leather grow round and soft, and the leaves turned into feathers, and, being gilded before, continued gilded still; so it became a dove, and she harnessed it to her chariot….

….*(Hiatus valde deflendus in MS.)*….

The Episode of Bentley and Wotton

D AY BEING FAR spent, and the numerous forces of the Moderns half inclining to a retreat, there issued forth, from a squadron of their heavy-armed foot, a captain whose name was Bentley, the most deformed of all the Moderns; tall, but without shape or comeliness; large, but without strength or proportion. His armour was patched up of a thousand incoherent pieces, and the sound of it, as he marched, was loud and dry, like that made by the fall of a sheet of lead, which an Etesian wind blows suddenly down from the roof of some steeple. His helmet was of old rusty iron, but the vizor was brass, which, tainted by his breath, corrupted into copperas, nor wanted gall from the same fountain, so that, whenever provoked by anger or labour, an atramentous quality, of most malignant nature, was seen to distil from his lips. In his right hand he grasped a flail, and (that he might never be unprovided of an offensive weapon) a vessel full of ordure in his left. Thus completely armed, he advanced with a slow and heavy pace where the Modern chiefs were holding a consult upon the sum of things, who, as he came onwards, laughed to behold his crooked leg and humped shoulder, which his boot and armour, vainly endeavouring to hide, were forced to comply with and expose. The generals made use of him for his talent of railing, which, kept within government, proved frequently of great service to their cause, but, at other times, did more mischief than good; for, at the least touch of offence, and often without any at all, he would, like a wounded elephant, convert it against his leaders. Such, at this juncture, was the disposition of Bentley, grieved to see the enemy prevail, and dissatisfied with everybody's conduct but his own. He humbly gave the Modern generals to understand that he conceived, with great submission, they were all a pack of rogues, and fools, and confounded logger-heads, and illiterate whelps, and nonsensical scoundrels; that, if himself had been constituted general, those presumptuous dogs, the Ancients, would long before this have been beaten out of the field. "You," said he, "sit here idle, but when I, or any other valiant Modern kill an enemy, you are sure to seize the spoil. But I will not march one foot against the foe till you all swear to me that whomever I take or kill, his arms I shall quietly possess." Bentley having spoken thus, Scaliger, bestowing him a sour look, "Miscreant prater!" said he, "eloquent only in thine own eyes, thou railest without wit, or truth, or discretion. The malignity of thy temper perverteth nature; thy learning makes thee more barbarous; thy study of humanity more inhuman; thy converse among poets more grovelling, miry, and dull. All arts of civilising others render thee rude and untractable; courts have taught thee ill manners, and polite conversation has finished thee a pedant. Besides, a greater coward burdeneth not the army. But never despond; I pass my word, whatever spoil thou takest shall certainly be thy own; though I hope that vile carcase will first become a prey to kites and worms."

Bentley durst not reply, but, half choked with spleen and rage, withdrew, in full resolution of performing some great achievement. With him, for his aid and companion, he took his beloved Wotton, resolving by policy or surprise to attempt some neglected quarter of the Ancients' army. They began their march over carcases of their slaughtered friends; then to the right of their own forces; then wheeled northward, till they came to Aldrovandus's tomb, which they passed on the side of the declining sun. And now they arrived, with fear, toward the enemy's out-guards, looking about, if haply they might spy the quarters of the wounded, or some straggling sleepers, unarmed and remote from the rest. As when two mongrel curs, whom native greediness and domestic want provoke and join in partnership, though fearful, nightly to invade the folds of some rich grazier, they, with tails depressed and lolling tongues, creep soft and slow. Meanwhile the conscious moon, now in her zenith, on their guilty heads darts perpendicular rays; nor dare they bark, though much provoked at her refulgent visage, whether seen in puddle by reflection or in sphere direct; but one surveys the region round, while the other scouts the plain, if haply to discover, at distance from the flock, some carcase half devoured, the refuse of gorged wolves or ominous ravens. So marched this lovely, loving pair of friends, nor with less fear and circumspection, when at a distance they might perceive two shining suits of armour hanging upon an oak, and the owners not far off in a profound sleep. The two friends drew lots, and the pursuing of this adventure fell to Bentley; on he went, and in his van Confusion and Amaze, while Horror and Affright brought up the rear. As he came near, behold two heroes of the Ancient army, Phalaris and Æsop, lay fast asleep. Bentley would fain have despatched them both, and, stealing close, aimed his flail at Phalaris's breast; but then the goddess Affright, interposing, caught the Modern in her icy arms, and dragged him from the danger she foresaw; both the dormant heroes happened to turn at the same instant, though soundly sleeping, and busy in a dream. For Phalaris was just that minute dreaming how a most vile poetaster had lampooned him, and how he had got him roaring in his bull. And Æsop dreamed that as he and the Ancient were lying on the ground, a wild ass broke loose, ran about, trampling and kicking in their faces. Bentley, leaving the two heroes asleep, seized on both their armours, and withdrew in quest of his darling Wotton.

He, in the meantime, had wandered long in search of some

enterprise, till at length he arrived at a small rivulet that issued from a fountain hard by, called, in the language of mortal men, Helicon. Here he stopped, and, parched with thirst, resolved to allay it in this limpid stream. Thrice with profane hands he essayed to raise the water to his lips, and thrice it slipped all through his fingers. Then he stopped prone on his breast, but, ere his mouth had kissed the liquid crystal, Apollo came, and in the channel held his shield betwixt the Modern and the fountain, so that he drew up nothing but mud. For, although no fountain on earth can compare with the clearness of Helicon, yet there lies at bottom a thick sediment of slime and mud; for so Apollo begged of Jupiter, as a punishment to those who durst attempt to taste it with unhallowed lips, and for a lesson to all not to draw too deep or far from the spring.

At the fountain-head Wotton discerned two heroes; the one he could not distinguish, but the other was soon known for Temple, general of the allies to the Ancients. His back was turned, and he was employed in drinking large draughts in his helmet from the fountain, where he had withdrawn himself to rest from the toils of the war. Wotton, observing him, with quaking knees and trembling hands, spoke thus to himself: O that I could kill this destroyer of our army, what renown should I purchase among the chiefs! but to issue out against him, man against man, shield against shield, and lance against lance, what Modern of us dare? for he fights like a god, and Pallas or Apollo are ever at his elbow. But, O mother! if what Fame reports be true, that I am the son of so great a goddess, grant me to hit Temple with this lance, that the stroke may send him to hell, and that I may return in safety and triumph, laden with his spoils. The first part of this prayer the gods granted at the intercession of his mother and of Momus; but the rest, by a perverse wind sent from Fate, was scattered in the air. Then Wotton grasped his lance, and, brandishing it thrice over his head, darted it with all his might; the goddess, his mother, at the same time adding strength to his arm. Away the lance went hizzing, and reached even to the belt of the averted Ancient, upon which, lightly grazing, it fell to the ground. Temple neither felt the weapon touch him nor heard it fall: and Wotton might have escaped to his army, with the honour of having remitted his lance against so great a leader unrevenged; but Apollo, enraged that a javelin flung by the assistance of so foul a goddess should pollute his fountain, put on the shape of—, and softly came to young Boyle, who then accompanied Temple: he pointed first to the lance, then to the distant Modern that flung it, and commanded the young hero to take immediate revenge. Boyle, clad in a suit of armour which had been given him by all the gods, immediately advanced against the trembling foe, who now fled before him. As a young lion in the Libyan plains, or Araby desert, sent by his aged sire to hunt for prey, or health, or exercise, he scours along, wishing to meet some tiger from the mountains, or a furious boar; if chance a wild ass, with brayings importune, affronts his ear, the generous beast, though loathing to distain his claws with blood so vile, yet, much provoked at the offensive noise, which Echo, foolish nymph, like her ill-judging sex, repeats much louder, and with more delight than Philomela's song, he vindicates the honour of the forest, and hunts the noisy long-eared animal. So Wotton fled, so Boyle pursued. But Wotton, heavy-armed, and slow of foot, began to slack his course, when his lover Bentley appeared, returning laden with the spoils of the two sleeping Ancients. Boyle observed him well, and soon discovering the helmet and shield of Phalaris his friend, both which he had lately with his own hands new polished and gilt, rage sparkled in his eyes, and, leaving his pursuit after Wotton, he furiously rushed on against this new approacher. Fain would he be revenged on both; but both now fled different ways: and, as a woman in a little house that gets a painful livelihood by spinning, if chance her geese be scattered o'er the common, she courses round the plain from side to side, compelling here and there the stragglers to the flock; they cackle loud, and flutter o'er the champaign; so Boyle pursued, so fled this pair of friends: finding at length their flight was vain, they bravely joined, and drew themselves in phalanx. First Bentley threw a spear with all his force, hoping to pierce the enemy's breast; but Pallas came unseen, and in the air took off the point, and clapped on one of lead, which, after a dead bang against the enemy's shield, fell blunted to the ground. Then Boyle, observing well his time, took up a lance of wondrous length and sharpness; and, as this pair of friends compacted, stood close side by side, he wheeled him to the right, and, with unusual force, darted the weapon. Bentley saw his fate approach, and flanking down his arms close to his ribs, hoping to save his body, in went the point, passing through arm and side, nor stopped or spent its force till it had also pierced the valiant Wotton, who, going to sustain his dying friend, shared his fate. As when a skilful cook has trussed a brace of woodcocks, he with iron skewer pierces the tender sides of both, their legs and wings close pinioned to the rib; so was this pair of friends transfixed, till down they fell, joined in their lives, joined in their deaths; so closely joined that Charon would mistake them both for one, and waft them over Styx for half his fare. Farewell, beloved, loving pair; few equals have you left behind: and happy and immortal shall you be, if all my wit and eloquence can make you.

And now....(*Desunt cætera*)....

A Meditation Upon a Broomstick

*According to the Style and Manner of the
Hon. Robert Boyle's Meditations.*

THIS SINGLE STICK, which you now behold ingloriously lying in that neglected corner, I once knew in a flourishing state in a forest. It was full of sap, full of leaves, and full of boughs; but now in vain does the busy art of man pretend to vie with nature, by tying that withered bundle of twigs to its sapless trunk; it is now at best but the reverse of what it was, a tree turned upside-down, the branches on the earth, and the root in the air; it is now handled by every dirty wench, condemned to do her drudgery, and, by a capricious kind of fate, destined to make other things clean, and be nasty itself; at length, worn to the stumps in the service of the maids, it is either thrown out of doors or condemned to the last use—of kindling a fire. When I behold this I sighed, and said within myself, *Surely mortal man is a broomstick!* Nature sent him into the world strong and lusty, in a thriving condition, wearing his own hair on his head, the proper branches of this reasoning vegetable, till the axe of intemperance has lopped off his green boughs, and left him a withered trunk; he then flies to art, and puts on a periwig, valuing himself upon an unnatural bundle of hairs, all covered with powder, that never grew on his head; but now should this our broomstick pretend to enter the scene, proud of those birchen spoils it never bore, and all covered with dust, through the sweepings of the finest lady's chamber, we should be apt to ridicule and despise its vanity. Partial judges that we are of our own excellencies, and other men's defaults!

But a broomstick, perhaps you will say, is an emblem of a tree standing on its head; and pray what is a man but a topsy-turvy creature, his animal faculties perpetually mounted on his rational, his head where his heels should be, grovelling on the earth? And yet, with all his faults, he sets up to be a universal reformer and corrector of abuses, a remover of grievances, rakes into every slut's corner of nature, bringing hidden corruptions to the light, and raises a mighty dust where there was none before, sharing deeply all the while in the very same pollutions he pretends to sweep away. His last days are spent in slavery to women, and generally the least deserving; till, worn to the stumps, like his brother besom, he is either kicked out of doors, or made use of to kindle flames for others to warm themselves by.

Predictions for the Year 1708

Wherein the Month, and Day of the Month are set down, the Persons named, and the great Actions and Events of next Year particularly related as will come to pass. Written to prevent the people of England from being farther imposed on by vulgar Almanack-makers.

By Isaac Bickerstaff, Esq.

I HAVE LONG CONSIDERED the gross abuse of astrology in this kingdom, and upon debating the matter with myself, I could not possibly lay the fault upon the art, but upon those gross impostors who set up to be the artists. I know several learned men have contended that the whole is a cheat; that it is absurd and ridiculous to imagine the stars can have any influence at all upon human actions, thoughts, or inclinations; and whoever has not bent his studies that way may be excused for thinking so, when he sees in how wretched a manner that noble art is treated by a few mean illiterate traders between us and the stars, who import a yearly stock of nonsense, lies, folly, and impertinence, which they offer to the world as genuine from the planets, though they descend from no greater a height than their own brains.

I intend in a short time to publish a large and rational defence of this art, and therefore shall say no more in its justification at present than that it hath been in all ages defended by many learned men, and among the rest by Socrates himself, whom I look upon as undoubtedly the wisest of uninspired mortals:

to which if we add that those who have condemned this art, though otherwise learned, having been such as either did not apply their studies this way, or at least did not succeed in their applications, their testimony will not be of much weight to its disadvantage, since they are liable to the common objection of condemning what they did not understand.

Nor am I at all offended, or think it an injury to the art, when I see the common dealers in it, the students in astrology, the Philomaths, and the rest of that tribe, treated by wise men with the utmost scorn and contempt; but rather wonder, when I observe gentlemen in the country, rich enough to serve the nation in Parliament, poring in Partridge's Almanack to find out the events of the year at home and abroad, not daring to propose a hunting-match till Gadbury or he have fixed the weather.

I will allow either of the two I have mentioned, or any other of the fraternity, to be not only astrologers, but conjurers too, if I do not produce a hundred instances in all their almanacks to convince any reasonable man that they do not so much as understand common grammar and syntax; that they are not able to spell any word out of the usual road, nor even in their prefaces write common sense or intelligible English. Then for their observations and predictions, they are such as will equally suit any age or country in the world. "This month a certain great person will be threatened with death or sickness." This the newspapers will tell them; for there we find at the end of the year that no month passes without the death of some person of note; and it would be hard if it should be otherwise, when there are at least two thousand persons of note in this kingdom, many of them old, and the almanack-maker has the liberty of choosing the sickliest season of the year where he may fix his prediction. Again, "This month an eminent clergyman will be preferred;" of which there may be some hundreds, half of them with one foot in the grave. Then "such a planet in such a house shows great machinations, plots, and conspiracies, that may in time be brought to light:" after which, if we hear of any discovery, the astrologer gets the honour; if not, his prediction still stands good. And at last, "God preserve King William from all his open and secret enemies, Amen." When if the King should happen to have died, the astrologer plainly foretold it; otherwise it passes but for the pious ejaculation of a loyal subject; though it unluckily happened in some of their almanacks that poor King William was prayed for many months after he was dead, because it fell out that he died about the beginning of the year.

To mention no more of their impertinent predictions: what have we to do with their advertisements about pills and drink for disease? or their mutual quarrels in verse and prose of Whig and Tory, wherewith the stars have little to do?

Having long observed and lamented these, and a hundred other abuses of this art, too tedious to repeat, I resolved to proceed in a new way, which I doubt not will be to the general satisfaction of the kingdom. I can this year produce but a specimen of what I design for the future, having employed most part of my time in adjusting and correcting the calculations I made some years past, because I would offer nothing to the world of which I am not as fully satisfied as that I am now alive. For these two last years I have not failed in above one or two particulars, and those of no very great moment. I exactly foretold the miscarriage at Toulon, with all its particulars, and the loss of Admiral Shovel, though I was mistaken as to the day, placing that accident about thirty-six hours sooner than it happened; but upon reviewing my schemes, I quickly found the cause of that error. I likewise foretold the Battle of Almanza to the very day and hour, with the lose on both sides, and the consequences thereof. All which I showed to some friends many months before they happened—that is, I gave them papers sealed up, to open at such a time, after which they were at liberty to read them; and there they found my predictions true in every article, except one or two very minute.

As for the few following predictions I now offer the world, I forbore to publish them till I had perused the several almanacks for the year we are now entered on. I find them all in the usual strain, and I beg the reader will compare their manner with mine. And here I make bold to tell the world that I lay the whole credit of my art upon the truth of these predictions; and I will be content that Partridge, and the rest of his clan, may hoot me for a cheat and impostor if I fail in any single particular of moment. I believe any man who reads this paper will look upon me to be at least a person of as much honesty and understanding as a common maker of almanacks. I do not lurk in the dark; I am not wholly unknown in the world; I have set my name at length, to be a mark of infamy to mankind, if they shall find I deceive them.

In one thing I must desire to be forgiven, that I talk more sparingly of home affairs. As it will be imprudence to discover secrets of State, so it would be dangerous to my person; but in smaller matters, and that are not of public consequence, I shall be very free; and the truth of my conjectures will as much appear from those as the others. As for the most signal events abroad, in France, Flanders, Italy, and Spain, I shall make no scruple to predict them in plain terms. Some of them are of importance, and I hope I shall seldom mistake the day they will happen; therefore I think good to inform the reader that I all along make use of the Old Style observed in England, which I desire he will compare with that of the newspapers at the time they relate the actions I mention.

I must add one word more. I know it hath been the opinion of several of the learned, who think well enough of the true art of astrology, that the stars do only incline, and not force the actions or wills of men, and therefore, however I may proceed by right rules, yet I cannot in prudence so confidently assure the events will follow exactly as I predict them.

I hope I have maturely considered this objection, which in some cases is of no little weight. For example: a man may, by the influence of an over-ruling planet, be disposed or inclined to lust, rage, or avarice, and yet by the force of reason overcome that bad influence; and this was the case of Socrates. But as the great events of the world usually depend upon numbers of men, it cannot be expected they should all unite to cross their inclinations from pursuing a general design wherein they unanimously agree. Besides, the influence of the stars reaches to many actions and events which are not any way in the power of reason, as sickness, death, and what we commonly call accidents, with many more, needless to repeat.

But now it is time to proceed to my predictions, which I have begun to calculate from the time that the sun enters into Aries. And this I take to be properly the beginning of the natural year. I pursue them to the time that he enters Libra, or somewhat more, which is the busy period of the year. The remainder I have not yet adjusted, upon account of several impediments needless here to mention. Besides, I must remind the reader again that this is but a specimen of what I design in succeeding years to treat more at large, if I may have liberty and encouragement.

My first prediction is but a trifle, yet I will mention it, to show how ignorant those sottish pretenders to astrology are in their own concerns. It relates to Partridge, the almanack-maker. I have consulted the stars of his nativity by my own rules, and find he will infallibly die upon the 29th of March next, about eleven at night, of a raging fever; therefore I advise him to consider of it, and settle his affairs in time.

The month of *April* will be observable for the death of many great persons. On the 4th will die the Cardinal de Noailles, Archbishop of Paris; on the 11th, the young Prince of Asturias, son to the Duke of Anjou; on the 14th, a great peer of this realm will die at his country house; on the 19th, an old layman of great fame for learning, and on the 23rd, an eminent goldsmith in Lombard Street. I could mention others, both at home and abroad, if I did not consider it is of very little use or instruction to the reader, or to the world.

As to public affairs: On the 7th of this month there will be an insurrection in Dauphiny, occasioned by the oppressions of the people, which will not be quieted in some months.

On the 15th will be a violent storm on the south-east coast of France, which will destroy many of their ships, and some in the very harbour.

The 11th will be famous for the revolt of a whole province or kingdom, excepting one city, by which the affairs of a certain prince in the Alliance will take a better face.

May, against common conjectures, will be no very busy month in Europe, but very signal for the death of the Dauphin, which will happen on the 7th, after a short fit of sickness, and grievous torments with the strangury. He dies less lamented by the Court than the kingdom.

On the 9th a Marshal of France will break his leg by a fall from his horse. I have not been able to discover whether he will then die or not.

On the 11th will begin a most important siege, which the eyes of all Europe will be upon: I cannot be more particular, for in relating affairs that so nearly concern the Confederates, and consequently this kingdom, I am forced to confine myself for several reasons very obvious to the reader.

On the 15th news will arrive of a very surprising event, than which nothing could be more unexpected.

On the 19th three noble ladies of this kingdom will, against all expectation, prove with child, to the great joy of their husbands.

On the 23rd a famous buffoon of the playhouse will die a ridiculous death, suitable to his vocation.

June. This month will be distinguished at home by the utter dispersing of those ridiculous deluded enthusiasts commonly called the Prophets, occasioned chiefly by seeing the time come that many of their prophecies should be fulfilled, and then finding themselves deceived by contrary events. It is indeed to be admired how any deceiver can be so weak to foretell things near at hand, when a very few months must of necessity discover the impostor to all the world; in this point less prudent than common almanack-makers, who are so wise to wonder in generals, and talk dubiously, and leave to the reader the business of interpreting.

On the 1st of this month a French general will be killed by a random shot of a cannon-ball.

On the 6th a fire will break out in the suburbs of Paris, which will destroy above a thousand houses, and seems to be the foreboding of what will happen, to the surprise of all Europe, about the end of the following month.

On the 10th a great battle will be fought, which will begin at four of the clock in the afternoon, and last till nine at night with great obstinacy, but no very decisive event. I shall not name the place, for the reasons aforesaid, but the commanders on each left wing will be killed. I see bonfires and hear the noise of guns for a victory.

On the 14th there will be a false report of the French king's death.

On the 20th Cardinal Portocarero will die of a dysentery, with great suspicion of poison, but the report of his intention to revolt to King Charles will prove false.

July. The 6th of this month a certain general will, by a glorious action, recover the reputation he lost by former misfortunes.

On the 12th a great commander will die a prisoner in the hands of his enemies.

On the 14th a shameful discovery will be made of a French Jesuit giving poison to a great foreign general; and when he is put to the torture, will make wonderful discoveries.

In short, this will prove a month of great action, if I might have liberty to relate the particulars.

At home, the death of an old famous senator will happen on the 15th at his country house, worn with age and diseases.

But that which will make this month memorable to all posterity is the death of the French king, Louis the Fourteenth, after a week's sickness at Marli, which will happen on the 29th, about six o'clock in the evening. It seems to be an effect of the gout in his stomach, followed by a flux. And in three days after Monsieur Chamillard will follow his master, dying suddenly of an apoplexy.

In this month likewise an ambassador will die in London, but I cannot assign the day.

August. The affairs of France will seem to suffer no change for a while under the Duke of Burgundy's administration; but the genius that animated the whole machine being gone, will be the cause of mighty turns and revolutions in the following year. The new king makes yet little change either in the army or the Ministry, but the libels against his grandfather, that fly about his very Court, give him uneasiness.

I see an express in mighty haste, with joy and wonder in his looks, arriving by break of day on the 26th of this month, having travelled in three days a prodigious journey by land and sea. In the evening I hear bells and guns, and see the blazing of a thousand bonfires.

A young admiral of noble birth does likewise this month gain immortal honour by a great achievement.

The affairs of Poland are this month entirely settled; Augustus resigns his pretensions which he had again taken up for some time: Stanislaus is peaceably possessed of the throne, and the King of Sweden declares for the emperor.

I cannot omit one particular accident here at home: that near the end of this month much mischief will be done at Bartholomew Fair by the fall of a booth.

September. This month begins with a very surprising fit of frosty weather, which will last near twelve days.

The Pope, having long languished last month, the swellings in his legs breaking, and the flesh mortifying, will die on the 11th instant; and in three weeks' time, after a mighty contest, be succeeded by a cardinal of the Imperial faction, but native of Tuscany, who is now about sixty-one years old.

The French army acts now wholly on the defensive, strongly fortified in their trenches, and the young French king sends overtures for a treaty of peace by the Duke of Mantua; which, because it is a matter of State that concerns us here at home, I shall speak no farther of it.

I shall add but one prediction more, and that in mystical terms, which shall be included in a verse out of Virgil—

Alter erit jam Tethys, et altera quæ vehat Argo
Delectos Heroas.

Upon the 25th day of this month, the fulfilling of this prediction will be manifest to everybody.

This is the farthest I have proceeded in my calculations for the present year. I do not pretend that these are all the great events which will happen in this period, but that those I have set down will infallibly come to pass. It will perhaps still be objected why I have not spoken more particularly of affairs at home, or of the success of our armies abroad, which I might, and could very largely have done; but those in power have wisely discouraged men from meddling in public concerns, and I was resolved by no means to give the least offence. This I will venture to say, that it will be a glorious campaign for the Allies, wherein the English forces, both by sea and land, will have their full share of honour; that Her Majesty Queen Anne will continue in health and prosperity; and that no ill accident will arrive to any in the chief Ministry.

As to the particular events I have mentioned, the readers may judge by the fulfilling of them, whether I am on the level with common astrologers, who, with an old paltry cant, and a few pothooks for planets, to amuse the vulgar, have, in my opinion, too long been suffered to abuse the world. But an honest physician ought not to be despised because there are such things as mountebanks. I hope I have some share of reputation, which I would not willingly forfeit for a frolic or humour; and I believe no gentleman who reads this paper will look upon it to be of the same cast or mould with the common scribblers that are every day hawked about. My fortune has placed me above the little regard of scribbling for a few pence, which I neither value nor want; therefore, let no wise man too hastily condemn this essay, intended for a good design, to cultivate and improve an ancient art long in disgrace, by having fallen into mean and unskilful hands. A little time will determine whether I have deceived others or myself; and I think it is no very unreasonable request that men would please to suspend their judgments till then. I was once of the opinion with those who despise all predictions from the stars, till in the year 1686 a man of quality showed me, written in his album, that the most learned astronomer, Captain Halley, assured him, he would never believe anything of the stars' influence if there were not a great revolution in England in the year 1688. Since that time I began to have other thoughts, and after eighteen years' diligent study and application, I think I have no reason to repent of my pains. I shall detain the reader no longer than to let him know that the account I design to give of next year's events shall take in the principal affairs that happen in Europe; and if I be denied the liberty of offering it to my own country, I shall appeal to the learned world, by publishing it in Latin, and giving order to have it printed in Holland.

An Argument Against Abolishing Christianity

*An argument to prove that the abolishing of Christianity in England may,
as things now stand, be attended with some inconveniences, and perhaps
not produce those many good effects proposed thereby.*

Written in the year 1708.

I AM VERY SENSIBLE what a weakness and presumption it is to
reason against the general humour and disposition of the
world. I remember it was with great justice, and a due regard to
the freedom, both of the public and the press, forbidden upon
several penalties to write, or discourse, or lay wagers against
the— even before it was confirmed by Parliament; because
that was looked upon as a design to oppose the current of the
people, which, besides the folly of it, is a manifest breach of
the fundamental law, that makes this majority of opinions the
voice of God. In like manner, and for the very same reasons, it
may perhaps be neither safe nor prudent to argue against the
abolishing of Christianity, at a juncture when all parties seem so
unanimously determined upon the point, as we cannot but allow
from their actions, their discourses, and their writings. However,
I know not how, whether from the affectation of singularity, or
the perverseness of human nature, but so it unhappily falls out,
that I cannot be entirely of this opinion. Nay, though I were
sure an order were issued for my immediate prosecution by
the Attorney-General, I should still confess, that in the present
posture of our affairs at home or abroad, I do not yet see the

absolute necessity of extirpating the Christian religion from among us.

This perhaps may appear too great a paradox even for our wise and paxodoxical age to endure; therefore I shall handle it with all tenderness, and with the utmost deference to that great and profound majority which is of another sentiment.

And yet the curious may please to observe, how much the genius of a nation is liable to alter in half an age. I have heard it affirmed for certain by some very odd people, that the contrary opinion was even in their memories as much in vogue as the other is now; and that a project for the abolishing of Christianity would then have appeared as singular, and been thought as absurd, as it would be at this time to write or discourse in its defence.

Therefore I freely own, that all appearances are against me. The system of the Gospel, after the fate of other systems, is generally antiquated and exploded, and the mass or body of the common people, among whom it seems to have had its latest credit, are now grown as much ashamed of it as their betters; opinions, like fashions, always descending from those of quality to the middle sort, and thence to the vulgar, where at length they are dropped and vanish.

But here I would not be mistaken, and must therefore be so bold as to borrow a distinction from the writers on the other side, when they make a difference betwixt nominal and real Trinitarians. I hope no reader imagines me so weak to stand up in the defence of real Christianity, such as used in primitive times (if we may believe the authors of those ages) to have an influence upon men's belief and actions. To offer at the restoring of that, would indeed be a wild project: it would be to dig up foundations; to destroy at one blow all the wit, and half the learning of the kingdom; to break the entire frame and constitution of things; to ruin trade, extinguish arts and sciences, with the professors of them; in short, to turn our courts, exchanges, and shops into deserts; and would be full as absurd as the proposal of Horace, where he advises the Romans, all in a body, to leave their city, and seek a new seat in some remote part of the world, by way of a cure for the corruption of their manners.

Therefore I think this caution was in itself altogether unnecessary (which I have inserted only to prevent all possibility of cavilling), since every candid reader will easily understand my discourse to be intended only in defence of nominal Christianity, the other having been for some time wholly laid aside by general consent, as utterly inconsistent with all our present schemes of wealth and power.

But why we should therefore cut off the name and title of Christians, although the general opinion and resolution be so violent for it, I confess I cannot (with submission) apprehend the consequence necessary. However, since the undertakers propose such wonderful advantages to the nation by this project, and advance many plausible objections against the system of Christianity, I shall briefly consider the strength of both, fairly allow them their greatest weight, and offer such answers as I think most reasonable. After which I will beg leave to show what inconveniences may possibly happen by such an innovation, in the present posture of our affairs.

First, one great advantage proposed by the abolishing of Christianity is, that it would very much enlarge and establish liberty of conscience, that great bulwark of our nation, and of the Protestant religion, which is still too much limited by priestcraft, notwithstanding all the good intentions of the legislature, as we have lately found by a severe instance. For it is confidently reported, that two young gentlemen of real hopes, bright wit, and profound judgment, who, upon a thorough examination of causes and effects, and by the mere force of natural abilities, without the least tincture of learning, having made a discovery that there was no God, and generously communicating their thoughts for the good of the public, were some time ago, by an unparalleled severity, and upon I know not what obsolete law, broke for blasphemy. And as it has been wisely observed, if persecution once begins, no man alive knows how far it may reach, or where it will end.

In answer to all which, with deference to wiser judgments, I think this rather shows the necessity of a nominal religion among us. Great wits love to be free with the highest objects; and if they cannot be allowed a god to revile or renounce, they will speak evil of dignities, abuse the government, and reflect upon the ministry, which I am sure few will deny to be of much more pernicious consequence, according to the saying of Tiberius, *deorum offensa diis curæ*. As to the particular fact related, I think it is not fair to argue from one instance, perhaps another cannot be produced: yet (to the comfort of all those who may be apprehensive of persecution) blasphemy we know is freely spoke a million of times in every coffee-house and tavern, or wherever else good company meet. It must be allowed, indeed, that to break an English free-born officer only for blasphemy was, to speak the gentlest of such an action, a very high strain of absolute power. Little can be said in excuse for the general; perhaps he was afraid it might give offence to the allies, among whom, for aught we know, it may be the custom of the country to believe a God. But if he argued, as some have done, upon a mistaken principle, that an officer who is guilty of speaking blasphemy may, some time or other, proceed so far as to raise a mutiny, the consequence is by no means to be admitted: for surely the commander of an English army is like to be but ill obeyed whose soldiers fear and reverence him as little as they do a Deity.

It is further objected against the Gospel system that it obliges men to the belief of things too difficult for Freethinkers, and such who have shook off the prejudices that usually cling to a confined education. To which I answer, that men should be cautious how they raise objections which reflect upon the wisdom of the nation. Is not everybody freely allowed to believe whatever he pleases, and to publish his belief to the world whenever he thinks fit, especially if it serves to strengthen the party which is in the right? Would any indifferent foreigner, who should read the trumpery lately written by Asgil, Tindal, Toland, Coward, and forty more, imagine the Gospel to be our rule of faith, and to be confirmed by Parliaments? Does any man either believe, or say he believes, or desire to have it thought that he says he believes, one syllable of the matter? And is any man worse received upon that score, or does he find his want of nominal faith a disadvantage to him in the pursuit of any civil or military employment? What if there be an old dormant statute or two against him, are they not now obsolete, to a degree, that Empson and Dudley themselves, if they were now alive, would find it impossible to put them in execution?

It is likewise urged, that there are, by computation, in this kingdom, above ten thousand parsons, whose revenues, added to those of my lords the bishops, would suffice to maintain at least two hundred young gentlemen of wit and pleasure, and free-thinking, enemies to priestcraft, narrow principles, pedantry, and prejudices, who might be an ornament to the court and town: and then again, so a great number of able [bodied] divines might be a recruit to our fleet and armies. This indeed appears to be a consideration of some weight; but then, on the other side, several things deserve to be considered likewise: as, first, whether it may not be thought necessary that in certain tracts of country, like what we call parishes, there should be one man at least of abilities to read and write. Then it seems a wrong computation that the revenues of the Church throughout this island would be large enough to maintain two hundred young gentlemen, or even half that number, after the present refined way of living, that is, to allow each of them such a rent as, in the modern form of speech, would make them easy. But still there is in this project a greater mischief behind; and we ought to beware of the woman's folly, who killed the hen that every morning laid her a golden egg. For, pray what would become of the race of men in the next age, if we had nothing to trust to beside the scrofulous consumptive production furnished by our men of wit and pleasure, when, having squandered away their vigour, health, and estates, they are forced, by some disagreeable marriage, to piece up their broken fortunes, and entail rottenness and politeness on their posterity? Now, here are ten thousand persons reduced, by the wise regulations of Henry VIII., to the necessity of a low diet, and moderate exercise, who are the only great restorers of our breed, without which the nation would in an age or two become one great hospital.

Another advantage proposed by the abolishing of Christianity is the clear gain of one day in seven, which is now entirely lost, and consequently the kingdom one seventh less considerable in trade, business, and pleasure; besides the loss to the public of so many stately structures now in the hands of the clergy, which might be converted into play-houses, exchanges, market-houses, common dormitories, and other public edifices.

I hope I shall be forgiven a hard word if I call this a perfect cavil. I readily own there hath been an old custom, time out of mind, for people to assemble in the churches every Sunday, and that shops are still frequently shut, in order, as it is conceived, to preserve the memory of that ancient practice; but how this can prove a hindrance to business or pleasure is hard to imagine. What if the men of pleasure are forced, one day in the week, to game at home instead of the chocolate-house? Are not the taverns and coffee-houses open? Can there be a more convenient season for taking a dose of physic? Is not that the chief day for traders to sum up the accounts of the week, and for lawyers to prepare their briefs? But I would fain know how it can be pretended that the churches are misapplied? Where are more appointments and rendezvouses of gallantry? Where more care to appear in the foremost box, with greater advantage of dress? Where more meetings for business? Where more bargains driven of all sorts? And where so many conveniences or incitements to sleep?

There is one advantage greater than any of the foregoing, proposed by the abolishing of Christianity, that it will utterly extinguish parties among us, by removing those factious distinctions of high and low church, of Whig and Tory, Presbyterian and Church of England, which are now so many mutual clogs upon public proceedings, and are apt to prefer the gratifying themselves or depressing their adversaries before the most important interest of the State.

I confess, if it were certain that so great an advantage would redound to the nation by this expedient, I would submit, and be silent; but will any man say, that if the words, whoring, drinking, cheating, lying, stealing, were, by Act of Parliament, ejected out of the English tongue and dictionaries, we should all awake next morning chaste and temperate, honest and just, and lovers of truth? Is this a fair consequence? Or if the physicians would forbid us to pronounce the words pox, gout, rheumatism, and stone, would that expedient serve like so many talismen to destroy the diseases themselves? Are party and faction rooted in men's hearts no deeper than phrases borrowed from religion, or founded upon no firmer principles? And is our language so poor that we cannot find other terms to express them? Are envy, pride, avarice, and ambition such ill nomenclators, that they cannot furnish appellations for their owners? Will not heydukes and mamalukes, mandarins and patshaws, or any other words formed at pleasure, serve to distinguish those who are in the ministry from others who would be in it if they could? What, for instance, is easier than to vary the form of speech, and instead of the word church, make it a question in politics, whether the monument be in danger? Because religion was nearest at hand to furnish a few convenient phrases, is our invention so barren we can find no other? Suppose, for argument sake, that the Tories favoured Margarita, the Whigs, Mrs. Tofts, and the Trimmers, Valentini, would not Margaritians, Toftians, and Valentinians be very tolerable marks of distinction? The Prasini and Veniti, two most virulent factions in Italy, began, if I remember right, by a distinction of colours in ribbons, which we might do with as good a grace about the dignity of the blue and the green, and serve as properly to divide the Court, the Parliament, and the kingdom between them, as any terms of art whatsoever, borrowed from religion. And therefore I think there is little force in this objection against Christianity, or prospect of so great an advantage as is proposed in the abolishing of it.

It is again objected, as a very absurd, ridiculous custom, that a set of men should be suffered, much less employed and hired, to bawl one day in seven against the lawfulness of those methods most in use towards the pursuit of greatness, riches, and pleasure, which are the constant practice of all men alive on the other six. But this objection is, I think, a little unworthy so refined an age as ours. Let us argue this matter calmly. I appeal to the breast of any polite Free-thinker, whether, in the pursuit of gratifying a pre-dominant passion, he hath not always felt a wonderful incitement, by reflecting it was a thing forbidden; and therefore we see, in order to cultivate this test, the wisdom of the nation hath taken special care that the ladies should be furnished with prohibited silks, and the men with prohibited wine. And indeed it were to be wished that some other prohibitions were promoted, in order to improve the pleasures of the town, which, for want of such expedients, begin already, as I am told, to flag and grow languid, giving way daily to cruel inroads from the spleen.

'Tis likewise proposed, as a great advantage to the public, that if we once discard the system of the Gospel, all religion will of course be banished for ever, and consequently along with it those grievous prejudices of education which, under the names of conscience, honour, justice, and the like, are so apt to disturb the peace of human minds, and the notions whereof are so hard to be eradicated by right reason or free-thinking, sometimes during the whole course of our lives.

Here first I observe how difficult it is to get rid of a phrase which the world has once grown fond of, though the occasion that first produced it be entirely taken away. For some years past, if a man had but an ill-favoured nose, the deep thinkers of the age would, some way or other contrive to impute the cause to the prejudice of his education. From this fountain were said to be derived all our foolish notions of justice, piety, love of our country; all our opinions of God or a future state, heaven, hell, and the like; and there might formerly perhaps have been some pretence for this charge. But so effectual care hath been since taken to remove those prejudices, by an entire change in the methods of education, that (with honour I mention it to our polite innovators) the young gentlemen, who are now on the scene, seem to have not the least tincture left of those infusions, or string of those weeds, and by consequence the reason for abolishing nominal Christianity upon that pretext is wholly ceased.

For the rest, it may perhaps admit a controversy, whether the banishing all notions of religion whatsoever would be inconvenient for the vulgar. Not that I am in the least of opinion with those who hold religion to have been the invention of politicians, to keep the lower part of the world in awe by the fear of invisible powers; unless mankind were then very different from what it is now; for I look upon the mass or body of our people here in England to be as Freethinkers, that is to say, as staunch unbelievers, as any of the highest rank. But I conceive some scattered notions about a superior power to be of singular use for the common people, as furnishing excellent materials to keep children quiet when they grow peevish, and providing topics of amusement in a tedious winter night.

Lastly, it is proposed, as a singular advantage, that the abolishing of Christianity will very much contribute to the uniting of Protestants, by enlarging the terms of communion, so as to take in all sorts of Dissenters, who are now shut out of the pale upon account of a few ceremonies, which all sides confess to be things indifferent. That this alone will effectually answer the great ends of a scheme for comprehension, by opening a large noble gate, at which all bodies may enter; whereas the chaffering with Dissenters, and dodging about this or t'other ceremony, is but like opening a few wickets, and leaving them at jar, by which no more than one can get in at a time, and that not without stooping, and sideling, and squeezing his body.

To all this I answer, that there is one darling inclination of mankind which usually affects to be a retainer to religion, though she be neither its parent, its godmother, nor its friend. I mean the spirit of opposition, that lived long before Christianity, and can easily subsist without it. Let us, for instance, examine wherein the opposition of sectaries among us consists. We shall find Christianity to have no share in it at all. Does the Gospel anywhere prescribe a starched, squeezed countenance, a stiff formal gait, a singularity of manners and habit, or any affected forms and modes of speech different from the reasonable part of mankind? Yet, if Christianity did not lend its name to stand in the gap, and to employ or divert these humours, they must of necessity be spent in contraventions to the laws of the land, and disturbance of the public peace. There is a portion of enthusiasm assigned to every nation, which, if it hath not proper objects to work on, will burst out, and set all into a flame. If the quiet of a State can be bought by only flinging men a few ceremonies to devour, it is a purchase no wise man would refuse. Let the mastiffs amuse themselves about a sheep's skin stuffed with hay, provided it will keep them from worrying the flock. The institution of convents abroad seems in one point a strain of great wisdom, there being few irregularities in human passions which may not have recourse to vent themselves in some of those orders, which are so many retreats for the speculative, the melancholy, the proud, the silent, the politic, and the morose, to spend themselves, and evaporate the noxious particles; for each of whom we in this island are forced to provide a several sect of religion to keep them quiet; and whenever Christianity shall be abolished, the Legislature must find some other expedient to employ and entertain them. For what imports it how large a gate you open, if there will be always left a number who place a pride and a merit in not coming in?

Having thus considered the most important objections against Christianity, and the chief advantages proposed by the abolishing thereof, I shall now, with equal deference and submission to wiser judgments, as before, proceed to mention a few inconveniences that may happen if the Gospel should be repealed, which, perhaps, the projectors may not have sufficiently considered.

And first, I am very sensible how much the gentlemen of wit and pleasure are apt to murmur, and be choked at the sight of so many daggle-tailed parsons that happen to fall in their way, and offend their eyes; but at the same time, these wise reformers do not consider what an advantage and felicity it is for great wits to be always provided with objects of scorn and contempt, in order to exercise and improve their talents, and divert their spleen from falling on each other, or on themselves, especially when all this may be done without the least imaginable danger to their persons.

And to urge another argument of a parallel nature: if Christianity were once abolished, how could the Freethinkers, the strong reasoners, and the men of profound learning be able to find another subject so calculated in all points whereon to display their abilities? What wonderful productions of wit should we be deprived of from those whose genius, by continual practice, hath been wholly turned upon raillery and invectives against religion, and would therefore never be able to shine or distinguish themselves upon any other subject? We are daily complaining of the great decline of wit among as, and would we take away the greatest, perhaps the only topic we have left? Who would ever have suspected Asgil for a wit, or Toland for a philosopher, if the inexhaustible stock of Christianity had not been at hand to provide them with materials? What other subject through all art or nature could have produced Tindal for a profound author, or furnished him with readers? It is the wise choice of the subject that alone adorns and distinguishes the writer. For had a hundred such pens as these been employed on the side of religion, they would have immediately sunk into silence and oblivion.

Nor do I think it wholly groundless, or my fears altogether imaginary, that the abolishing of Christianity may perhaps bring the Church in danger, or at least put the Senate to the trouble of another securing vote. I desire I may not be mistaken; I am far from presuming to affirm or think that the Church is in danger at present, or as things now stand; but we know not how soon it may be so when the Christian religion is repealed. As plausible as this project seems, there may be a dangerous design lurk under it. Nothing can be more notorious than that the Atheists, Deists, Socinians, Anti-Trinitarians, and other subdivisions of Freethinkers, are persons of little zeal for the present ecclesiastical establishment: their declared opinion is for repealing the sacramental test; they are very indifferent with regard to ceremonies; nor do they hold the *Jus Divinum* of episcopacy: therefore they may be intended as one politic step towards altering the constitution of the Church established, and setting up Presbytery in the stead, which I leave to be further considered by those at the helm.

In the last place, I think nothing can be more plain, than that by this expedient we shall run into the evil we chiefly pretend to avoid; and that the abolishment of the Christian religion will be the readiest course we can take to introduce Popery. And I am the more inclined to this opinion because we know it has been the constant practice of the Jesuits to send over emissaries, with instructions to personate themselves members of the several prevailing sects amongst us. So it is recorded that they have at sundry times appeared in the guise of Presbyterians, Anabaptists, Independents, and Quakers, according as any of these were most in credit; so, since the fashion hath been taken up of exploding religion, the Popish missionaries have not been wanting to mix with the Freethinkers; among whom Toland, the great oracle of the Anti-Christians, is an Irish priest, the son of an Irish priest; and the most learned and ingenious author of a book called the "Rights of the Christian Church," was in a proper juncture reconciled to the Romish faith, whose true son, as appears by a hundred passages in his treatise, he still continues. Perhaps I could add some others to the number; but the fact is beyond dispute, and the reasoning they proceed by is right: for supposing Christianity to be extinguished the people will never he at ease till they find out some other method of worship, which will as infallibly produce superstition as this will end in Popery.

And therefore, if, notwithstanding all I have said, it still be thought necessary to have a Bill brought in for repealing

Christianity, I would humbly offer an amendment, that instead of the word Christianity may be put religion in general, which I conceive will much better answer all the good ends proposed by the projectors of it. For as long as we leave in being a God and His Providence, with all the necessary consequences which curious and inquisitive men will be apt to draw from such promises, we do not strike at the root of the evil, though we should ever so effectually annihilate the present scheme of the Gospel; for of what use is freedom of thought if it will not produce freedom of action, which is the sole end, how remote soever in appearance, of all objections against Christianity? and therefore, the Freethinkers consider it as a sort of edifice, wherein all the parts have such a mutual dependence on each other, that if you happen to pull out one single nail, the whole fabric must fall to the ground. This was happily expressed by him who had heard of a text brought for proof of the Trinity, which in an ancient manuscript was differently read; he thereupon immediately took the hint, and by a sudden deduction of a long Sorites, most logically concluded: why, if it be as you say, I may safely drink on, and defy the parson. From which, and many the like instances easy to be produced, I think nothing can be more manifest than that the quarrel is not against any particular points of hard digestion in the Christian system, but against religion in general, which, by laying restraints on human nature, is supposed the great enemy to the freedom of thought and action.

Upon the whole, if it shall still be thought for the benefit of Church and State that Christianity be abolished, I conceive, however, it may be more convenient to defer the execution to a time of peace, and not venture in this conjuncture to disoblige our allies, who, as it falls out, are all Christians, and many of them, by the prejudices of their education, so bigoted as to place a sort of pride in the appellation. If, upon being rejected by them, we are to trust to an alliance with the Turk, we shall find ourselves much deceived; for, as he is too remote, and generally engaged in war with the Persian emperor, so his people would be more scandalised at our infidelity than our Christian neighbours. For they are not only strict observers of religions worship, but what is worse, believe a God; which is more than is required of us, even while we preserve the name of Christians.

To conclude, whatever some may think of the great advantages to trade by this favourite scheme, I do very much apprehend that in six months' time after the Act is passed for the extirpation of the Gospel, the Bank and East India stock may fall at least one per cent. And since that is fifty times more than ever the wisdom of our age thought fit to venture for the preservation of Christianity, there is no reason we should be at so great a loss merely for the sake of destroying it.

A Discourse Concerning the Mechanical Operation of the Spirit

In a Letter to a Friend. A Fragment.

THE BOOKSELLER'S ADVERTISEMENT

THE FOLLOWING DISCOURSE came into my hands perfect and entire; but there being several things in it which the present age would not very well bear, I kept it by me some years, resolving it should never see the light. At length, by the advice and assistance of a judicious friend, I retrenched those parts that might give most offence, and have now ventured to publish the remainder. Concerning the author I am wholly ignorant; neither can I conjecture whether it be the same with that of the two foregoing pieces, the original having been sent me at a different time, and in a different hand. The learned reader will better determine, to whose judgment I entirely submit it.

A Discourse, &c.

For T. H. Esquire,[1] at his chambers in the Academy of the Beaux Esprits,
in New England.

S IR,—IT IS now a good while since I have had in my head
something, not only very material, but absolutely necessary
to my health, that the world should be informed in; for, to tell
you a secret, I am able to contain it no longer. However, I have
been perplexed for some time to resolve what would be the
most proper form to send it abroad in. To which end I have
been three days coursing through Westminster Hall, and St.
Paul's churchyard, and Fleet Street, to peruse titles; and I do
not find any which holds so general a vogue as that of a Letter
to a Friend: nothing is more common than to meet with long
epistles addressed to persons and places where, at first thinking,
one would be apt to imagine it not altogether so necessary or
convenient; such as, a neighbour at next door, a mortal enemy, a
perfect stranger, or a person of quality in the clouds; and these
upon subjects, in appearance, the least proper for conveyance
by the post; as long schemes in philosophy, dark and wonderful
mysteries of state, laborious dissertations in criticism and philosophy, advice to parliaments, and the like.

Now, sir, to proceed after the method in present wear; for, let

---

1   Supposed to be Col. Hunter, believed to be the author of the *Letter of
Enthusiasm*. See *Tale of a Tub*, p. 13. (W.S.) This Discourse is not altogether
equal to the former, the best parts of it being omitted; whether the bookseller's
account be true, that he durst not print the rest, I know not; nor indeed is it
easy to determine, whether he may be relied on in anything he says of this or
the former treatises. (J.S.)

me say what I will to the contrary, I am afraid you will publish this letter as soon as ever it comes to your hand. I desire you will be my witness to the world how careless and sudden a scribble it has been; that it was but yesterday when you and I began accidentally to fall into discourse on this matter; that I was not very well when we parted; that the post is in such haste I have had no manner of time to digest it into order or correct the style; and if any other modern excuses for haste and negligence shall occur to you in reading, I beg you to insert them, faithfully promising they shall be thankfully acknowledged.

Pray, sir, in your next letter to the Iroquois virtuosi, do me the favour to present my humble service to that illustrious body, and assure them I shall send an account of those phenomena as soon as we can determine them at Gresham.

I have not had a line from the literati of Topinambou these three last ordinaries.

And now, sir, having despatched what I had to say of form or of business, let me entreat you will suffer me to proceed upon my subject, and to pardon me if I make no farther use of the epistolary style till I come to conclude.

Section I

It is recorded of Mahomet that, upon a visit he was going to pay in Paradise, he had an offer of several vehicles to conduct him upwards; as fiery chariots, winded horses, and celestial sedans; but he refused them all, and would be borne to heaven upon nothing but his ass. Now this inclination of Mahomet, as singular as it seems, has been since taken up by a great number of devout Christians, and doubtless with very good reason. For, since that Arabian is known to have borrowed a moiety of his religious system from the Christian faith, it is but just he should pay reprisals to such as would challenge them; wherein the good people of England, to do them all right, have not been backward; for, though there is not any other nation in the world so plentifully provided with carriages for that journey, either as to safety or ease, yet there are abundance of us who will not be satisfied with any other machine beside this of Mahomet.

For my own part, I must confess to bear[2] a very singular respect to this animal, by whom I take human nature to be most admirably held forth in all its qualities, as well as operations; and therefore, whatever in my small reading occurs concerning this our fellow-creature, I do never fail to set it down by way of commonplace; and when I have occasion to write upon human reason, politics, eloquence, or knowledge, I lay my memorandums before me, and insert them with a wonderful facility of application. However, among all the qualifications ascribed to this distinguished brute, by ancient or modern authors, I cannot remember this talent of bearing his rider to heaven has been recorded for a part of his character, except in the two examples mentioned already; therefore I conceive the methods of this art to be a point of useful knowledge in very few hands, and which the learned world would gladly be better informed in: this is what I have undertaken to perform in the following discourse. For towards the operation already mentioned many peculiar properties are required both in the rider and the ass, which I shall endeavour to set in as clear a light as I can.

But, because I am resolved, by all means, to avoid giving offence to any party whatever, I will leave off discoursing so closely to the letter as I have hitherto done, and go on for the future by way of allegory; though in such a manner that the judicious reader may, without much straining, make his applications as often as he shall think fit. Therefore, if you please, from henceforward, instead of the term ass, we shall make use

---

2 This is a very singular mode of expression, it should be, 'I must confess that I bear,' &c.

of gifted or enlightened teacher; and the word rider we will exchange for that of fanatic auditory, or any other denomination of the like import. Having settled this weighty point, the great subject of inquiry before us is to examine by what methods this teacher arrives at his gifts, or spirit, or light; and by what intercourse between him and his assembly it is cultivated and supported.

In all my writings I have had constant regard to this great end, not to suit and apply them to particular occasions and circumstances of time, of place, or of person, but to calculate them for universal nature and mankind in general. And of such catholic use I esteem this present disquisition;[3] for I do not remember any other temper of body, or quality of mind, wherein all nations and ages of the world have so unanimously agreed as that of a fanatic strain or tincture of enthusiasm; which, improved by certain persons or societies of men, and by them practised upon the rest, has been able to produce revolutions of the greatest figure in history, as will soon appear to those who know anything of Arabia, Persia, India, or China, of Morocco and Peru. Farther, it has possessed as great a power in the kingdom of knowledge, where it is hard to assign one art or science which has not annexed to it some fanatic branch; such are, the philosopher's stone, the grand elixir,[4] the planetary worlds, the squaring of the circle, the *summum bonum*, Utopian commonwealths, with some others of less or subordinate note, which all serve for nothing else but to employ or amuse this grain of enthusiasm dealt into every composition.

But if this plant has found a root in the fields of empire and of knowledge, it has fixed deeper and spread yet farther upon holy ground; wherein, though it has passed under the general

---

3   This sentence is defective, for want of the words, 'to be,' at the end of it: as thus, 'and of such catholick use I esteem this present disquisition to be.'
4   Some writers hold them for the same, others not.

name of enthusiasm, and perhaps arisen from the same original, yet has it produced certain branches of a very different nature, however often mistaken for each other. The word, in its universal acceptation, may be defined, a lifting up of the soul, or its faculties, above matter. This description will hold good in general, but I am only to understand it as applied to religion; wherein there are three general ways of ejaculating the soul, or transporting it beyond the sphere of matter. The first is the immediate act of God, and is called prophecy or inspiration. The second is the immediate act of the devil, and is termed possession. The third is the product of natural causes, the effect of strong imagination, spleen, violent anger, fear, grief, pain, and the like. These three have been abundantly treated on by authors, and therefore shall not employ my inquiry. But the fourth method of religious enthusiasm, or launching out of the soul, as it is purely an effect of artifice and mechanic operation, has been sparingly handled, or not at all, by any writer; because, though it is an art of great antiquity, yet, having been confined to few persons, it long wanted those advancements and refinements which it afterwards met with, since it has grown so epidemic, and fallen into so many cultivating hands.

It is therefore upon this mechanical operation of the spirit that I mean to treat, as it is at present performed by our British workmen. I shall deliver to the reader the result of many judicious observations upon the matter; tracing, as near as I can, the whole course and method of this trade, producing parallel instances and relating certain discoveries that have luckily fallen in my way.

I have said that there is one branch of religious enthusiasm which is purely an effect of nature; whereas the part I mean to handle is wholly an effect of art, which however is inclined to work upon certain natures and constitutions more than others. Besides, there is many an operation which in its original was purely an artifice, but through a long succession of ages has grown to be natural. Hippocrates tells us that among our ancestors the Scythians there was a nation called Long-heads, which at first began[5] by a custom among midwives and nurses of moulding, and squeezing, and bracing up the heads of infants; by which means nature, shut out at one passage, was forced to seek another, and, finding room above, shot upwards in the form of a sugar-loaf; and, being diverted that way for some generations, at last found it out of herself, needing no assistance from the nurse's hand. This was the original of the Scythian Long-heads, and thus did custom, from being a second nature, proceed to be a first. To all which there is something very analogous among us of this nation, who are the undoubted posterity of that refined people. For in the age of our fathers there arose a generation of men in this island called round-heads,[6] whose race is now spread over three kingdoms; yet in its beginning was merely an operation of art produced by a pair of scissors, a squeeze of the face, and a black cap. These heads, thus formed into a perfect sphere in all assemblies, were most exposed to the view of the female sort, which did influence their conceptions so effectually, that nature at last took the hint and did it of herself; so that a round-head has been ever since as familiar a sight among us as a long-head among the Scythians.

Upon these examples, and others easy to produce, I desire the curious reader to distinguish, first, between an effect grown

---

5   Which at first began, &c. as, 'which,' refers here to the word, 'nation,' in the preceding part of the sentence, this does not make sense: it should be thus — 'there was a nation called 'Long-heads', which name took its rise from a custom among 'midwives,' &c.

6   The fanaticks in the time of Charles I, ignorantly applying the text, 'Ye know that it is a shame for men to have long hair,' cut their's very short. It is said, that the queen once seeing Pym, a celebrated patriot, thus cropped, inquired who that round-headed man was, and that from this incident the distinction became general, and the party were called round-heads.

from art into nature, and one that is natural from its beginning: secondly, between an effect wholly natural, and one which has only a natural foundation, but where the superstructure is entirely artificial. For the first and the last of these I understand to come within the districts of my subject. And having obtained these allowances, they will serve to remove any objections that may be raised hereafter against what I shall advance.

The practitioners of this famous art proceed, in general, upon the following fundamental: that the corruption of the senses is the generation of the spirit; because the senses in men are so many avenues to the fort of reason, which in this operation is wholly blocked up. All endeavours must be therefore used, either to divert, bind up, stupify, fluster, and amuse the senses, or else to justle them out of their stations; and, while they are either absent or otherwise employed, or engaged in a civil war against each other, the spirit enters and performs its part.

Now, the usual methods of managing the senses upon such conjunctures are, what I shall be very particular in delivering, as far as it is lawful for me to do; but, having had the honour to be initiated into the mysteries of every society, I desire to be excused from divulging any rites wherein the profane must have no part.

But here, before I can proceed farther, a very dangerous objection must if possible be removed. For it is positively denied by certain critics that the spirit can, by any means, be introduced into an assembly of modern saints; the disparity being so great in many material circumstances between the primitive way of inspiration and that which is practised in the present age. This they pretend to prove from the second chapter of the Acts, where, comparing both, it appears, first, that the apostles were gathered together with one accord, in one place; by which is meant a universal agreement in opinion and form of worship; a harmony, say they, so far from being found between any two conventicles among us, that it is in vain to expect it between any two heads in the same. Secondly, the spirit instructed the apostles in the gift of speaking several languages; a knowledge so remote from our dealers in this art, that they neither understand propriety of words or phrases in their own. Lastly, say these objectors, the modern artists do utterly exclude all approaches of the spirit, and bar up its ancient way of entering, by covering themselves so close and so industriously a-top: for they will needs have it as a point clearly gamed, that the cloven tongues never sat upon the apostles' heads while their hats were on.

Now, the force of these objections seems to consist in the different acceptation of the word spirit; which,[7] if it be understood for a supernatural assistance approaching from without, the objectors have reason, and their assertions may be allowed; but the spirit we treat of here proceeding entirely from within, the argument of these adversaries is wholly eluded. And upon the same account, our modern artificers find it an expedient of absolute necessity to cover their heads as close as they can in order to prevent perspiration, than which nothing is observed to be a greater spender of mechanic light, as we may perhaps further show in a convenient place.

To proceed therefore upon the phenomenon of spiritual mechanism, it is here to be noted that in forming and working up the spirit the assembly has a considerable share as well as the preacher. The method of this arcanum is as follows: they violently strain their eyeballs inward, half closing the lids; then, as they sit, they are in a perpetual motion of see-saw, making long hums at proper periods, and continuing the sound at equal height, choosing their time in those intermissions while the preacher is at ebb. Neither is this practice in any part of

---

7   This is wholly ungrammatical; the nominative 'which' has no verb in the sentence afterwards to which it refers, and may be omitted without prejudice to the sense.

it so singular and improbable as not to be traced in distant regions from reading and observation. For, first, the Jauguis,[8] or enlightened saints of India, see all their visions by help of an acquired straining and pressure of the eyes. Secondly, the art of see-saw on a beam, and swinging by session upon a cord, in order to raise artificial ecstasies, has been derived to us from our Scythian[9] ancestors, where it is practised at this day among the women. Lastly, the whole proceeding, as I have here related it, as performed by the natives of Ireland with a considerable improvement; and it is granted that this noble nation has, of all others, admitted fewer corruptions and degenerated least from the purity of the old Tartars. Now, it is usual for a knot of Irish men and women to abstract themselves from matter, bind up all their senses, grow visionary and spiritual, by influence of a short pipe of tobacco handed round the company, each preserving the smoke in his mouth till it comes again to his turn to take in fresh; at the same time there is a concert of a continued gentle hum, repeated and renewed by instinct as occasion requires; and they move their bodies up and down to a degree that sometimes their heads and points lie parallel to the horizon. Meanwhile you may observe their eyes turned up, in the posture of one who endeavours to keep himself awake; by which, and many other symptoms among them, it manifestly appears that the reasoning faculties are all suspended and superseded, that imagination has usurped the seat, scattering a thousand deliriums over the brain. Returning from this digression, I shall describe the methods by which the spirit approaches. The eyes being disposed according to art, at first you can see nothing; but after a short pause a small glimmering light begins to appear and dance before you : then, by frequently moving your body up and down, you perceive the vapours to ascend very fast, till you are perfectly dosed and

8   Bernier, Mem. de Mogol
9   Guagnini Hist. Sarmat.

flustered like one who drinks too much in a morning. Meanwhile the preacher is also at work; he begins a loud hum which pierces you quite through; this is immediately returned by the audience, and you find yourself prompted to imitate them by a mere spontaneous impulse, without knowing what you do. The *interstitia* are duly filled up by the preacher to prevent too long a pause, under which the spirit would soon faint and grow languid.

This is all I am allowed to discover about the progress of the spirit with relation to that part which is borne by the assembly; but in the methods of the preacher to which I now proceed I shall be more large and particular.

Section II

You will read it very gravely remarked in the books of those illustrious and right eloquent penmen, the modern travellers, that the fundamental difference in point of religion between the wild Indians and us, lies in this—that we worship God, and they worship the devil. But there are certain critics who will by no means admit of this distinction, rather believing that all nations whatsoever adore the true God, because they seem to intend their devotions to some invisible power of greatest goodness and ability to help them; which perhaps will take in the brightest attributes ascried to the Divinity. Others again inform us that those idolaters adore two principles—the principle of good, and that of evil; which indeed I am apt to look upon as the most universal notion that mankind, by the mere light of nature, ever entertained of things invisible. How this idea has been managed by the Indians and us, and with what advantage to the understandings of either, may well deserve to be examined. To me the difference appears little more than this, that they are put oftener upon their knees by their fears, and we by our desires; that the former set them a praying, and us a cursing. What I applaud them for is, their discretion in limiting their devotions and their deities to their several districts, nor ever suffering the liturgy of the white God to cross or to interfere with that of the black. Not so with us, who, pretending by the lines and measures of our reason to extend the dominion of one invisible power, and contract that of the other, have discovered a gross ignorance in the natures of good and evil, and most horribly confounded the frontiers of both. After men have lifted up the throne of their divinity to the *coelum empyroeum,* adorned with all such qualities and accomplishments as themselves seem most to value and possess—after they have sunk their principle of evil to the lowest centre, bound him with chains, loaded him with curses, furnished him with viler dispositions than any rake-hell of the town, accoutred him with tail, and horns, and huge claws, and saucer eyes—I laugh aloud to see these reasoners at the same time engaged in wise dispute, about certain walks and purlieus, whether they are in the verge of God or the devil; seriously debating whether such and such influences come into men's minds from above or below; whether certain passions and affections are guided by the evil spirit or the good:

> Dum fas atqne ncfas exiguo fine libidinum
> Discernunt avidi.

Thus do men establish a fellowship of Christ with Belial, and such is the analogy they make between cloven tongues and cloven feet. Of the like nature is the disquisition before us: it has continued these hundred years an even debate whether the deportment and the cant of our English enthusiastic preachers were possession or inspiration; and a world of argument has been drained on either side, perhaps to little purpose. For I think it is in life as in tragedy, where it is held a conviction of great defect, both in order and invention, to interpose the assistance of preternatural power without an absolute and last necessity. However, it is a sketch of human vanity for every individual to imagine the whole universe is interested in his meanest concern. If he has got cleanly over a kennel, some angel unseen descended on purpose to help him by the hand; if he has knocked his head against a post, it was the devil for his sins let loose from hell on purpose to buffet him. Who that .sees a little paltry mortal, droning, and dreaming, and drivelling to a multitude, can think it agreeable to common good sense that either heaven or hell should lie put to the trouble of influence or inspection upon what he is about? therefore I am resolved immediately to weed this error out of mankind, by making it clear that this mystery of vending spiritual gifts is nothing but a trade, acquired by as much instruction, and mastered by equal practice and application, as others are. This will best appear by describing and deducting the whole process of the operation, as variously as it hath fallen under my knowledge or experience.

[Here the whole scheme of spiritual mechanism teas deduced arid explained, with an appearance of great reading and observation; but it was thought neither safe nor convenient to print it.]

Here it may not be amiss to add a few words upon the laudable practice of wearing quilted caps; which is not a matter of mere custom, humour, or fashion, as some would pretend, but an institution of great sagacity and use: these, when moistened with sweat, stop all perspiration; and, by reverberating the heat, prevent the spirit from evaporating any way but at the mouth; even as a skilful housewife that covers her still with a wet clout for the same reason, and finds the same effect. For it is the opinion of choice *virtuosi* that the brain is only a crowd of little animals, but with teeth and claws extremely sharp, and therefore cling together in the contexture we behold, like the picture of

Hobbes' *Leviathan*, or like bees in perpendicular swarm upon a tree, or like a carrion corrupted into vermin, still preserving the shape and figure of the mother animal: that all invention is formed by the morsure of two or more of these animals upon certain capillary nerves which proceed from thence, whereof three branches spread into the tongue, and two into the right hand. They hold also that these animals arc of a constitution extremely cold; that their food is the air we attract, their excrement phlegm; and that what we vulgarly call rheums, and colds, and distillations, is nothing else but an epidemical looseness, to which that little commonwealth is very subject from the climate it lies under. Further, that nothing less than a violent heat can disentangle these creatures from their hamated station of life, or give them vigour and humour to imprint the marks of their little teeth. That if the morsure be hexagonal it produces poetry; the circular gives eloquence; if the bite hath been conical, the person whose nerve is so affected shall be disposed to write upon politics; and so of the rest.

I shall now discourse briefly by what kind of practices the voice is best governed toward the composition and improvement of the spirit; for, without a competent skill in tuning and toning each word, and syllable, and letter, to their due cadence, the whole operation is incomplete, misses entirely of its effect on the hearers, and puts the workman himself to continual pains for new supplies, without success. For it is to be understood that, in the language of the spirit, cant and droning supply the place of sense and reason in the language of men: because, in spiritual harangues, the disposition of the words according to the art of grammar has not the least use, but the skill and influence wholly lie in the choice and cadence of the syllables; even as a discreet composer, who, in setting a song, changes the words and order so often, that he is forced to make it nonsense before he can make it music. For this reason it has been held by some that the art of canting is ever in greatest perfection when managed by ignorance; which is thought to be enigmatically meant by Plutarch, when he tells us that the best musical instruments were made from the bones of an ass. And the profounder critics upon that passage are of opinion, the word, in its genuine signification, means no other than a jaw-bone; though some rather think it to have been the *os sacrum;* but in so nice a case I shall not take upon me to decide; the curious are at liberty to pick from it whatever they please.

The first ingredient toward the art of canting is, a competent share of inward light; that is to say, a large memory, plentifully fraught with theological polysyllables and mysterious texts from holy writ, applied and digested by those methods and mechanical operations already related: the bearers of this light resembling lanterns compact of leaves from old Geneva bibles; which invention, Sir Humphrey Edwin,[10] during his mayoralty, of happy memory, highly approved and advanced; affirming the Scripture to be now fulfilled, where it says. Thy word is a lantern to my feet, and a light to my paths.

Now, the art of canting consists in skilfully adapting the voice to whatever words the spirit delivers, that each may strike the ears of the audience with its most significant cadence. The force or energy of this eloquence is not to be found, as among ancient orators, in the disposition of words to a sentence, or the turning of long periods; but, agreeably to the modern refinements in music, is taken up wholly in dwelling and dilating upon syllables and letters. Thus, it is frequent for a single vowel to draw sighs from a multitude, and for a whole assembly of saints to sob to the music of one solitary liquid. But these are trifles, when even sounds inarticulate are observed to produce as forcible effects. A master workman shall blow his nose so powerfully as

---

10   A Presbyterian, who, ascending to the dignity of Lord Mayor of London, went in his official character to a meeting-house. —W.S.

to pierce the hearts of his people, who were disposed to receive the excrements of his brain with the same reverence as the issue of it. Hawking, spitting, and belching, the defects of other men's rhetoric, are the flowers, and figures, and ornaments of his. For the spirit being the same in all, it is of no import through what vehicle it is conveyed.

It is a point of too much difficulty to draw the principles of this famous art within the compass of certain adequate rules. However, perhaps I may one day oblige the world with my critical essay upon the art of canting; philosophically, physically, and musically considered.

But, among all improvements of the spirit, wherein the voice has borne a part, there is none to be compared with that of conveying the sound through the nose, which, under the denomination of snuffling,[11] has passed with so great applause in the world. The originals of this institution are very dark: but, having been initiated into the mystery of it, and leave being given me to publish it to the world, I shall deliver as direct a relation as I can.

This art, like many other famous inventions, owed its birth, or at least improvement and perfection, to an effect of chance; but was established upon solid reasons, and has flourished in this island ever since with great lustre. All agree that it first appeared upon the decay and discouragement of bagpipes, which, having long suffered under the mortal hatred of the brethren, tottered for a time, and at last fell with monarchy. The story is thus related.

As yet snuffling was not, when the following adventure happened to a Banbury saint. Upon a certain day, while he was far engaged among the tabernacles of the wicked, he felt the

---

11 The snuffling of men, who have lost their noses by lewd courses, is said to have given rise to that tone, which our dissenters did too much affect. W. Wotton.

outward man put into odd commotions, and strangely pricked forward by the inward; an effect very usual among the modern inspired. For some think that the spirit is apt to feed on the flesh, like hungry wines upon raw beef. Others rather believe there is a perpetual game at leap-frog between both; and sometimes the flesh is uppermost, and sometimes the spirit; adding that the former, while it is in the state of a rider, wears huge Rippon spurs; and, when it comes to the turn of being bearer, is wonderfully headstrong and hardmouthed. However it came about, the saint felt his vessel full extended in every part; (a very natural effect of strong inspiration); and the place and time falling out so unluckily that he could not have the convenience of evacuating upwards, by repetition, prayer, or lecture, he was forced to open can inferior vent. In short, he wrestled with the flesh so long, that he at length subdued it, coming off with honourable wounds call before. The surgeon had now cured the parts primarily affected; but the disease, driven from its post, flew up into his head; and, as a skilful general, valiantly attacked in his trenches, and beaten from the field, by flying marches withdraws to the capital city, breaking down the bridges to prevent pursuit; so the disease, repelled from its first station, fled before the rod of Hermes to the upper region, there fortifying itself; but, finding the foe making attacks at the nose, broke down the bridge and retired to the headquarters. Now, the naturalists observe that there is in human noses an idiosyncrasy, by virtue of which, the more the passage is obstructed, the more our speech delights to go through, as the music of a flageolet is made by the stops. By this method the twang of the nose becomes perfectly to resemble the snuffle of a bagpipe, and is found to be equally attractive of British ears; whereof the saint had sudden experience, by practising his new faculty with wonderful success, in the operation of the spirit: for, in a short time, no doctrine passed for sound and orthodox unless it were delivered through the nose. Straight every pastor copied after this original; and those who could not otherwise arrive to a perfection, spirited by a noble zeal, made use of the same experiment to acquire it; so that, I think, it may be truly affirmed the saints owe their empire to the snuffling of one animal, as Darius did his to the neighing of another; and both stratagems were performed by the same art; for we read how the Persian beast acquired his faculty by covering a mare the day before.[12]

I should now have done, if I were not convinced that whatever I have yet advanced upon this subject is liable to great exception. For, allowing all I have said to be true, it may still be justly objected that there is in the commonwealth of artificial enthusiasm some real foundation for art to work upon, in the temper and complexion of individuals, which other mortals seem to want. Observe but the gesture, the motion, and the countenance of some choice professors, though in their most familiar actions, you will find them of a different race from the rest of human creatures. Remark your commonest pretender to a light within, how dark, and dirty, and gloomy he is without; as lanterns, which, the more light they bear in their bodies, cast out so much the more soot, and smoke, and fuliginous matter to adhere to the sides. Listen but to their ordinary talk, and look on the mouth that delivers it, you will imagine you are hearing some ancient oracle, and your understanding will be equally informed. Upon these, and the like reasons, certain objectors pretend to put it beyond all doubt that there must be a sort of preternatural spirit possessing the heads of the modern saints; and some will have it to be the heat of zeal working upon the dregs of ignorance, as other spirits arc produced from lees by the force of fire. Some again think, that when our earthly tabernacles are disordered and desolate, shaken and out of repair,

---

12 Herodotus.

the spirit delights to dwell within them; as houses are said to be haunted when they are forsaken and gone to decay.

To set this matter in as fair a light as possible, I shall here very briefly deduce the history of fanaticism from the most early ages to the present. And if we are able fix upon any one material or fundamental point, wherein the chief professors have universally agreed, I think we may reasonably lay hold on that, and assign it for the great seed or principle of the spirit.

The most early traces we meet with of fanatics in ancient story are among the Egyptians, who instituted those rites known in Greece by the names of Orgia, Panegyres and Dionysia; whether introduced there by Orpheus or Melampus we shall not dispute at present, nor in all likelihood at any time for the future.[13] These feasts were celebrated to the honour of Osiris, whom the Grecians called Dionysius, and is the same with Bacchus: which has betrayed some superficial readers to imagine that the whole business was nothing more than a set of roaring, scouring companions, overcharged with wine; but this is a scandalous mistake, foisted on the world by a sort of modern authors, who have too literal an understanding; and, because antiquity is to be traced backwards, do therefore, like Jews, begin their books at the wrong end, as if learning were a sort of conjuring. These are the men who pretend to understand a book by scouring through the index; as if a traveller should go about to describe a palace, when he had seen nothing but the privy; or like certain fortune-tellers in Northern America, who have a way of reading a man's destiny by peeping into his breech. For, at the time of instituting these mysteries, there was not one vine in all Egypt,[14] the natives drinking nothing but ale; which liquor seems to have been far more ancient than wine, and has the honour of owing its invention and progress,

13   Diod. Sic. L. I. Plut. de Iside & Osiride.
14   Herodotus, 1. ii.

not only to the Egyptian Osiris,[15] but to the Grecian Bacchus; who, in their famous expedition, carried the receipt of it along with them, and gave it to the nations they visited or subdued. Besides, Bacchus himself was very seldom or never drunk; for it is recorded of him that he was the first inventor of the mitre,[16] which he wore continually on his head (as the whole company of bacchanals did), to prevent vapours and the headache after hard drinking. And for this reason, say some, the scarlet whore, when she makes the kings of the earth drunk with her cup of abomination, is always sober herself, though she never balks the glass in her turn, being, it seems, kept upon her legs by the virtue of her triple mitre. Now these feasts were instituted in imitation of the famous expedition Osiris made through the world, and of the company that attended him, whereof the bacchanalian ceremonies were so many types and symbols. From which account[17] it is manifest that the fanatic rites of these bacchanals cannot be imputed to intoxications by wine, but must needs have had a deeper foundation. What this was, we may gather large hints from certain circumstances in the course of their mysteries. For, in the first place, there was, in their processions, an entire mixture and confusion of sexes; they affected to ramble about hills and deserts; their garlands were of ivy and vine, emblems of cleaving and clinging; or of fir, the parent of turpentine. It is added that they imitated satyrs, were attended by goats, and rode upon asses, all companions of great skill and practice in affairs of gallantry. They bore for their ensigns certain curious figures, perched upon long poles, made into the shape and size of the *virga genitalis*, with its appurtenances; which were so many shadows and emblems of the whole mystery, as well as trophies set up by the female conquerors. Lastly, in a

---

15   Diod. Sic. L. 1 and 3.
16   Id. L. 4.
17   See the particulars in Diod. Sic. L. 1 and 3.

certain town of Attica, the whole solemnity, stripped of all its types,[18] was performed *in puris naturalibus,* the votaries not flying in coveys, but sorted into couples. The same may be further conjectured from the death of Orpheus, one of the institutors of these mysteries, who was torn in pieces by women, because he refused to communicate his orgies to them;[19] which others explained by telling us he had castrated himself upon grief for the loss of his wife.

Omitting many others of less note, the next fanatics we meet with of any eminence were the numerous sects of heretics appearing in the five first centuries of the Christian era, from Simon Magus and his followers to those of Eutyches. I have collected their systems from infinite reading, and, comparing them with those of their successors in the several ages since, I find there are certain bounds set even to the irregularity of human thought, and those a great deal narrower than is commonly apprehended. For, as they all frequently interfere even in their wildest ravings, so there is one fundamental point wherein they are sure to meet, as lines in a centre, and that is, the community of women. Great were their solicitudes in this matter, and they never failed of certain articles, in their schemes of worship, on purpose to establish it.

The last fanatics of note were those which started up in Germany a little after the reformation of Luther, springing as mushrooms do at the end of a harvest; such were John of Leyden, David George, Adam Neuster, and many others, whose visions and revelations always terminated in leading about half a dozen sisters a-piece, and making that practice a fundamental part of their system. For human life is a continual navigation, and if we expect our vessels to pass with safety through the waves and tempests of this fluctuating world, it is necessary to

---

18   Dionysia Brauronia.
19   Vid. Photium in excerptis è Conone.

make a good provision of the flesh, as seamen lay in store of beef for a long voyage.

Now, from this brief survey of some principal sects among the fanatics in all ages (having omitted the Mahometans and others, who might also help to confirm the argument I am about), to which I might add several among ourselves, such as the family of love, sweet singers of Israel, and the like; and, from reflecting upon that fundamental point in their doctrines about women wherein they have so unanimously agreed, I am apt to imagine that the seed or principle which has ever put men upon visions in things invisible is of a corporeal nature; for the profounder chemists inform us that the strongest spirits may be extracted from human flesh. Besides, the spinal marrow, being nothing else but a continuation of the brain, must needs create a very free communication between the superior faculties and those below; and thus the thorn in the flesh serves for a spur to the spirit. I think it is agreed among physicians that nothing affects the head so much as a tentiginous humour, repelled and elated to the upper region, found, by daily practice, to run frequently up into madness. A very eminent member of the faculty assured me that when the Quakers first appeared he seldom was without some female patients among them for the *furor* —; persons of a visionary devotion, either men or women, are, in their complexion, of all others, the most amorous; for zeal is frequently kindled from the same spark with other fires, and, from inflaming brotherly love, will proceed to raise that of a gallant. If we inspect into the usual process of modern courtship, we shall find it to consist in a devout turn of the eyes, called ogling; an artificial form of canting and whining by rote, every interval for want of other matter, made up with a shrug or a hum, a sigh or a groan; the style compact of insignificant words, incoherences, and repetition. These I take to be the most accomplished rules of address to a mistress; and where are these performed with more dexterity than by the saints? Nay, to bring this argument yet closer, I have been informed by certain sanguine brethren of the first class, that, in the height and orgasmus of their spiritual exercise, it has been frequent with them...; immediately after which, they found the spirit to relax and flag of a sudden with the nerves, and they were forced to hasten to a conclusion. This may be further strengthened by observing, with wonder, how unaccountably all females are attracted by visionary or enthusiastic preachers, though ever so contemptible in their outward mien; which is usually supposed to be done upon considerations purely spiritual, without any carnal regards at all. But I have reason to think the sex has certain characteristics, by which they form a truer judgment of human abilities and performings than we ourselves can possibly do of each other. Let that be as it will, thus much is certain, that, however spiritual intrigues begin, they generally conclude like all others; they may branch upward toward heaven, but the root is in the earth. Too intense a contemplation is not the business of flesh and blood; it must, by the necessary course of things, in a little time let go its hold, and fall into matter. Lovers for the sake of celestial converse are but another sort of Platonics, who pretend to see stars and heaven in ladies' eyes, and to look or think no lower; but the same pit is provided for both; and they seem a perfect moral to the story of that philosopher, who, while his thoughts and eyes were fixed upon the constellations, found himself seduced by his lower parts into a ditch.

I had somewhat more to say upon this part of the subject; but the post is just going, which forces me in great haste to conclude.

Sir, yours, etc.

Pray burn this letter as soon as it comes to your hands.

Hints Towards an Essay on Conversation

I HAVE OBSERVED FEW obvious subjects to have been so seldom, or at least so slightly, handled as this; and, indeed, I know few so difficult to be treated as it ought, nor yet upon which there seemeth so much to be said.

Most things pursued by men for the happiness of public or private life our wit or folly have so refined, that they seldom subsist but in idea; a true friend, a good marriage, a perfect form of government, with some others, require so many ingredients, so good in their several kinds, and so much niceness in mixing them, that for some thousands of years men have despaired of reducing their schemes to perfection. But in conversation it is or might be otherwise; for here we are only to avoid a multitude of errors, which, although a matter of some difficulty, may be in every man's power, for want of which it remaineth as mere an idea as the other. Therefore it seemeth to me that the truest way to understand conversation is to know the faults and errors to which it is subject, and from thence every man to form maxims to himself whereby it may be regulated, because it requireth few talents to which most men are not born, or at least may not acquire without any great genius or study. For nature bath left every man a capacity of being agreeable, though not of shining in company; and there are a hundred men sufficiently qualified for both, who, by a very few faults that they might correct in half an hour, are not so much as tolerable.

I was prompted to write my thoughts upon this subject by mere indignation, to reflect that so useful and innocent a pleasure, so fitted for every period and condition of life, and so much in all men's power, should be so much neglected and abused.

And in this discourse it will be necessary to note those errors that are obvious, as well as others which are seldomer observed, since there are few so obvious or acknowledged into which most men, some time or other, are not apt to run.

For instance, nothing is more generally exploded than the folly of talking too much; yet I rarely remember to have seen five people together where some one among them hath not been predominant in that kind, to the great constraint and disgust of all the rest. But among such as deal in multitudes of words, none are comparable to the sober deliberate talker, who proceedeth with much thought and caution, maketh his preface, brancheth out into several digressions, findeth a hint that putteth him in mind of another story, which he promiseth to tell you when this is done; cometh back regularly to his subject, cannot readily call to mind some person's name, holdeth his head, complaineth of his memory; the whole company all this while in suspense; at length, says he, it is no matter, and so goes on. And, to crown the business, it perhaps proveth at last a story the company hath heard fifty times before; or, at best, some insipid adventure of the relater.

Another general fault in conversation is that of those who affect to talk of themselves. Some, without any ceremony, will run over the history of their lives; will relate the annals of their diseases, with the several symptoms and circumstances of them; will enumerate the hardships and injustice they have suffered in court, in parliament, in love, or in law. Others are more dexterous, and with great art will lie on the watch to hook in their own praise. They will call a witness to remember they always foretold what would happen in such a case, but none would believe them; they advised such a man from the beginning, and told him the consequences just as they happened, but he would have his own way. Others make a vanity of telling their faults. They are the strangest men in the world; they cannot dissemble; they own it is a folly; they have lost abundance of advantages by it; but, if you would give them the world, they cannot help it; there is something in their nature that abhors insincerity and constraint; with many other unsufferable topics of the same altitude.

Of such mighty importance every man is to himself, and ready to think he is so to others, without once making this easy and obvious reflection, that his affairs can have no more weight with other men than theirs have with him; and how little that is he is sensible enough.

Where company hath met, I often have observed two persons discover by some accident that they were bred together at the same school or university, after which the rest are condemned to silence, and to listen while these two are refreshing each other's memory with the arch tricks and passages of themselves and their comrades.

I know a great officer of the army, who will sit for some time with a supercilious and impatient silence, full of anger and contempt for those who are talking; at length of a sudden demand audience; decide the matter in a short dogmatical way; then withdraw within himself again, and vouchsafe to talk no more, until his spirits circulate again to the same point.

There are some faults in conversation which none are so subject to as the men of wit, nor ever so much as when they are with each other. If they have opened their mouths without endeavouring to say a witty thing, they think it is so many words lost. It is a torment to the hearers, as much as to themselves, to see them upon the rack for invention, and in perpetual constraint, with so little success. They must do something extraordinary, in order to acquit themselves, and answer their character, else the standers by may be disappointed and be apt to think them only like the rest of mortals. I have known two men of wit industriously brought together, in order to entertain the company, where they have made a very ridiculous figure, and provided all the mirth at their own expense.

I know a man of wit, who is never easy but where he can be allowed to dictate and preside; he neither expecteth to be informed or entertained, but to display his own talents. His business is to be good company, and not good conversation, and therefore he chooseth to frequent those who are content to listen, and profess themselves his admirers. And, indeed, the worst conversation I ever remember to have heard in my life was that at Will's coffee-house, where the wits, as they were called, used formerly to assemble; that is to say, five or six men who had written plays, or at least prologues, or had share in a miscellany, came thither, and entertained one another with their trifling composures in so important an air, as if they had been the noblest efforts of human nature, or that the fate of kingdoms depended on them; and they were usually attended with a humble audience of young students from the inns of courts, or the universities, who, at due distance, listened to these oracles, and returned home with great contempt for their law and philosophy, their heads filled with trash under the name of politeness, criticism, and belles lettres.

By these means the poets, for many years past, were all over-run with pedantry. For, as I take it, the word is not properly used; because pedantry is the too front or unseasonable obtruding our own knowledge in common discourse, and placing too great a value upon it; by which definition men of the court or the army may be as guilty of pedantry as a philosopher or a divine; and it is the same vice in women when they are over copious upon the subject of their petticoats, or their fans, or their china. For which reason, although it be a piece of prudence, as well as good manners, to put men upon talking on subjects they are best versed in, yet that is a liberty a wise man could hardly take;

because, beside the imputation of pedantry, it is what he would never improve by.

This great town is usually provided with some player, mimic, or buffoon, who hath a general reception at the good tables; familiar and domestic with persons of the first quality, and usually sent for at every meeting to divert the company, against which I have no objection. You go there as to a farce or a puppet-show; your business is only to laugh in season, either out of inclination or civility, while this merry companion is acting his part. It is a business he hath undertaken, and we are to suppose he is paid for his day's work. I only quarrel when in select and private meetings, where men of wit and learning are invited to pass an evening, this jester should be admitted to run over his circle of tricks, and make the whole company unfit for any other conversation, besides the indignity of confounding men's talents at so shameful a rate.

Raillery is the finest part of conversation; but, as it is our usual custom to counterfeit and adulterate whatever is too dear for us, so we have done with this, and turned it all into what is generally called repartee, or being smart; just as when an expensive fashion cometh up, those who are not able to reach it content themselves with some paltry imitation. It now passeth for raillery to run a man down in discourse, to put him out of countenance, and make him ridiculous, sometimes to expose the defects of his person or understanding; on all which occasions he is obliged not to be angry, to avoid the imputation of not being able to take a jest. It is admirable to observe one who is dexterous at this art, singling out a weak adversary, getting the laugh on his side, and then carrying all before him. The French, from whom we borrow the word, have a quite different idea of the thing, and so had we in the politer age of our fathers. Raillery was, to say something that at first appeared a reproach or reflection, but, by some turn of wit unexpected and surprising, ended always in a compliment, and to the advantage of the person it was addressed to. And surely one of the best rules in conversation is, never to say a thing which any of the company can reasonably wish we had rather left unsaid; nor can there anything be well more contrary to the ends for which people meet together, than to part unsatisfied with each other or themselves.

There are two faults in conversation which appear very different, yet arise from the same root, and are equally blamable; I mean, an impatience to interrupt others, and the uneasiness of being interrupted ourselves. The two chief ends of conversation are, to entertain and improve those we are among, or to receive those benefits ourselves; which whoever will consider, cannot easily run into either of those two errors; because, when any man speaketh in company, it is to be supposed he doth it for his hearers' sake, and not his own; so that common discretion will teach us not to force their attention, if they are not willing to lend it; nor, on the other side, to interrupt him who is in possession, because that is in the grossest manner to give the preference to our own good sense.

There are some people whose good manners will not suffer them to interrupt you; but, what is almost as bad, will discover abundance of impatience, and lie upon the watch until you have done, because they have started something in their own thoughts which they long to be delivered of. Meantime, they are so far from regarding what passes, that their imaginations are wholly turned upon what they have in reserve, for fear it should slip out of their memory; and thus they confine their invention, which might otherwise range over a hundred things full as good, and that might be much more naturally introduced.

There is a sort of rude familiarity, which some people, by practising among their intimates, have introduced into their general conversation, and would have it pass for innocent freedom or humour, which is a dangerous experiment in our northern climate, where all the little decorum and politeness we have are purely forced by art, and are so ready to lapse into barbarity. This, among the Romans, was the raillery of slaves, of which we have many instances in Plautus. It seemeth to have been introduced among us by Cromwell, who, by preferring the scum of the people, made it a court-entertainment, of which I have heard many particulars; and, considering all things were turned upside down, it was reasonable and judicious; although it was a piece of policy found out to ridicule a point of honour in the other extreme, when the smallest word misplaced among gentlemen ended in a duel.

There are some men excellent at telling a story, and provided with a plentiful stock of them, which they can draw out upon occasion in all companies; and considering how low conversation runs now among us, it is not altogether a contemptible talent; however, it is subject to two unavoidable defects: frequent repetition, and being soon exhausted; so that whoever valueth this gift in himself hath need of a good memory, and ought frequently to shift his company, that he may not discover the weakness of his fund; for those who are thus endowed have seldom any other revenue, but live upon the main stock.

Great speakers in public are seldom agreeable in private conversation, whether their faculty be natural, or acquired by practice and often venturing. Natural elocution, although it may seem a paradox, usually springeth from a barrenness of invention and of words, by which men who have only one stock of notions upon every subject, and one set of phrases to express them in, they swim upon the superficies, and offer themselves on every occasion; therefore, men of much learning, and who know the compass of a language, are generally the worst talkers on a sudden, until much practice hath inured and emboldened them; because they are confounded with plenty of matter, variety of notions, and of words, which they cannot readily choose, but are perplexed and entangled by too great a choice, which is no disadvantage in private conversation; where, on the other side, the talent of haranguing is, of all others, most insupportable.

Nothing hath spoiled men more for conversation than the character of being wits; to support which, they never fail of encouraging a number of followers and admirers, who list themselves in their service, wherein they find their accounts on both sides by pleasing their mutual vanity. This hath given the former such an air of superiority, and made the latter so pragmatical, that neither of them are well to be endured. I say nothing here of the itch of dispute and contradiction, telling of lies, or of those who are troubled with the disease called the wandering of the thoughts, that they are never present in mind at what passeth in discourse; for whoever labours under any of these possessions is as unfit for conversation as madmen in Bedlam.

I think I have gone over most of the errors in conversation that have fallen under my notice or memory, except some that are merely personal, and others too gross to need exploding; such as lewd or profane talk; but I pretend only to treat the errors of conversation in general, and not the several subjects of discourse, which would be infinite. Thus we see how human nature is most debased, by the abuse of that faculty, which is held the great distinction between men and brutes; and how little advantage we make of that which might be the greatest, the most lasting, and the most innocent, as well as useful pleasure of life: in default of which, we are forced to take up with those poor amusements of dress and visiting, or the more pernicious ones of play, drink, and vicious amours, whereby the nobility and gentry of both sexes are entirely corrupted both in body and mind, and have lost all notions of love, honour, friendship, and generosity; which, under the name of fopperies, have been for some time laughed out of doors.

This degeneracy of conversation, with the pernicious

consequences thereof upon our humours and dispositions, hath been owing, among other causes, to the custom arisen, for some time past, of excluding women from any share in our society, further than in parties at play, or dancing, or in the pursuit of an amour. I take the highest period of politeness in England (and it is of the same date in France) to have been the peaceable part of King Charles I.'s reign; and from what we read of those times, as well as from the accounts I have formerly met with from some who lived in that court, the methods then used for raising and cultivating conversation were altogether different from ours; several ladies, whom we find celebrated by the poets of that age, had assemblies at their houses, where persons of the best understanding, and of both sexes, met to pass the evenings in discoursing upon whatever agreeable subjects were occasion-ally started; and although we are apt to ridicule the sublime Platonic notions they had, or personated in love and friendship, I conceive their refinements were grounded upon reason, and that a little grain of the romance is no ill ingredient to preserve and exalt the dignity of human nature, without which it is apt to degenerate into everything that is sordid, vicious, and low. If there were no other use in the conversation of ladies, it is sufficient that it would lay a restraint upon those odious topics of immodesty and indecencies, into which the rudeness of our northern genius is so apt to fall. And, therefore, it is observable in those sprightly gentlemen about the town, who are so very dexterous at entertaining a vizard mask in the park or the play-house, that, in the company of ladies of virtue and honour, they are silent and disconcerted, and out of their element.

There are some people who think they sufficiently acquit themselves and entertain their company with relating of facts of no consequence, nor at all out of the road of such common incidents as happen every day; and this I have observed more frequently among the Scots than any other nation, who are very careful not to omit the minutest circumstances of time or place; which kind of discourse, if it were not a little relieved by the uncouth terms and phrases, as well as accent and gesture peculiar to that country, would be hardly tolerable. It is not a fault in company to talk much; but to continue it long is certainly one; for, if the majority of those who are got together be naturally silent or cautious, the conversation will flag, unless it be often renewed by one among them who can start new subjects, provided he doth not dwell upon them, but leaveth room for answers and replies.

1667   Jonathan Swift is born on November 30 in Dublin, Ireland; he is the second child and only son of English parents. His father, a lawyer, dies of syphilis in the spring months before he is born. Swift's mother returns to England, leaving him in the care of his uncle, Godwin Swift, a close friend and confidant of Sir John Temple, the former Master of the Rolls in Ireland.

1668   Smuggled to Whitehaven, England, by his nurse, who travels there to attend the deathbed of a relative. When Swift's mother discovers what has happened, she sends instructions that, because of his delicate health, he isn't to risk the return journey until he is older. He spends nearly three years in Whitehaven in the care of his nurse.

1671   Nurse returns him to Ireland and the home of his benefactor and uncle, Godwin Swift.

1673   With his uncle's support, begins his formal education at Kilkenny, the best school in Ireland.

1682   Graduates from Kilkenny; attends Trinity College Dublin.

1686   An unexceptional student, Swift receives his B.A. from Trinity College Dublin "by special grace." Begins studying for a master's degree.

1688–89   William of Orange invades England. With Dublin in political turmoil, Trinity College is closed and Swift goes to England. His mother helps him secure a position as the secretary and personal assistant of Sir William Temple (son of Sir John Temple) at Moor Park, near Farnham, Surrey. Temple is a retired English diplomat, politician, and writer, and someone Swift comes to greatly admire and respect.

Becomes tutor and mentor to eight-year-old Esther Johnson. She is the daughter of a widow who is the companion to Temple's sister Lady Giffard. Swift nicknames her "Stella" and the two remain close for the rest of her life.

There nature of Swift's enduring relationship with Stella has become a subject of debate. Both Denis Johnston (1901–1984), an Irish writer who authored a full-length biography of Swift, and Michael Foot (1913–2010), a British politician who wrote extensively about Swift, subscribe to an hypothesis about Swift's parentage that bears upon his relationship with Stella. Johnston postulates that Swift's biological father was Sir William Temple's father, Sir John Temple. It is widely thought that Stella was Sir William Temple's illegitimate daughter. If true, Swift is the half-brother of Sir William Temple, his employer, and Stella's uncle.

1690   On his doctor's advice, Swift returns to Ireland after a first appearance of Ménière's disease, a disease of the inner ear.

1691   Swift, back with Temple in England, begins studying at Oxford.

Publishes first poem, "Ode to the Athenian Society."

1692   Receives an M.A. degree from Oxford for purposes of ordination.

1694   In Ireland, Swift takes deacon's orders.

1695	In January, ordained as a priest in the Church of Ireland, the Irish branch of the Anglican Church. Becomes prebendary of Kilroot, near Belfast.
	A surviving letter from Swift to Jane Waring, the sister of a college friend, contains a proposal of marriage and a vow to leave Ireland if she refuses, which she does.
1696–99	Swift returns to Moor Park in England, and composes most of *A Tale of a Tub*, his first great work.
	Temple dies on January 27, 1699. Swift stays in England to finish editing Temple's memoirs, which, when published, alienate him from members of Temple's family who object to its candor with regard to indiscretions.
	After failing to secure a suitable position in England, travels to Ireland to become secretary and chaplain to the Earl of Berkeley, one of the Lords Justice of Ireland. Upon arrival, however, he finds that the secretarial post has been filled.
1700	Becomes vicar of Laracor, Agher, and Rathbeggan, and the prebend of Dunlavin in St. Patrick's Cathedral, Dublin. He uses his abundant free time to write, cultivate his garden, and rebuild the vicarage. As chaplain to Lord Berkeley, he spends much of his time in Dublin and travels to London frequently over the next ten years.
1702	Swift receives Doctor of Divinity degree from Trinity College Dublin.
	Travels to England in the spring, returning to Ireland with Stella and Rebecca Dingley, another member of William Temple's household.
1704	Publication of *A Tale of a Tub* and *The Battle of the Books*.

Swift writes letter to Reverend William Tisdall object-ing to his intention of proposing marriage to Stella.

1707–09 Swift makes trips to London as emissary of Irish cler-gy urging claims to the First-Fruits and Twentieths ("Queen Anne's Bounty"), a scheme established in 1704 to augment the incomes of the poorer clergy of the Church of England. His requests are rejected by the Whig (later Liberal) government. The Tory (later Conservative) government is more amendable to his cause. Swift later describes himself as "a lover of liber-ty...a Whig in politics...But, as to religion, I confessed myself to be an High-Churchman."

Swift becomes intensely involved with Esther Vanhom-righ, who he nicknames "Vanessa." She is the daughter of Dutch merchants who had settled in Ireland. Their fraught relationship continues until her death in 1723.

In 1708, publishes *An Argument Against Abolishing Chris-tianity*.

1710 Swift's mother dies.

In England, Swift falls out with Whigs, formally allies himself with the Tories, and becomes editor of the pro-government newspaper, *The Examiner*.

Over the next three years, writes a series of letters that will be published posthumously as *A Journal to Stella*.

1713 Publication of the poem "Cadenus and Vanessa."

Swift is installed as Dean of St. Patrick's Cathedral in Dublin. He had hoped for an appointment in England, but his writings had provoked the ire of Queen Anne, who thwarts these efforts.

Returns to England in December.

1714   Founding member of Scriblerus Club, an informal association of London-based authors that includes Alexander Pope, John Gay, John Arbuthnot, and Thomas Parnell.

Queen Anne dies, George I takes the throne, the Tories fall from power. Swift's hopes for preferment in England come to an end and he returns to Ireland.

Vanessa follows him to Ireland and settles at her old family home, Celbridge Abbey. She is infatuated with Swift, whose feelings toward her had cooled.

1716   Many, notably his close friend Thomas Sheridan, believe that Swift and Stella secretly marry; others, like Swift's housekeeper Mrs. Brent and Rebecca Dingley (who lived with Stella during her years in Ireland), dismiss the story.

1718   Swift begins to publish tracts on Irish problems.

1720   Swift begins work on *Gulliver's Travels*, intended, as he says in a letter to Alexander Pope, "to vex the world, not to divert it."

1723   Vanessa's relationship with Swift ends; she dies shortly thereafter.

1724–25 Publication of *Drapier's Letters* under the pseudonym M. B., Drapier. They are widely known to be Swift's work, and gain him enormous popularity in Ireland. This series of pamphlets inveigh against the monopoly granted by the English government to William Wood to mint copper coinage for Ireland. After much public outcry, Wood's patent is rescinded in September of 1725 and the coins are kept out of circulation.

1726   Travels to England where he stays with close friends Alexander Pope, John Arbuthnot, and John Gay, who help him arrange for the publication of *Gulliver's Travels*.

Gulliver's Travels is published under a pseudonym, the fictional Lemuel Gulliver, a ship's surgeon and later a sea captain. It is an immediate, resounding success. French, German, and Dutch translations of *Gulliver's Travels* are published the following year.

1727   Swift's last trip to England, where he is hosted again by Alexander Pope. Returns to Ireland in haste when he receives word that Stella is dying.

Publication of first of multiple volumes of *Miscellanies in Prose and Verse* by Jonathan Swift, Alexander Pope, John Arbuthnot, and John Gay.

1728   Stella dies; Swift is inconsolable.

1729   Publication of *A Modest Proposal for Preventing the Children of Poor People in Ireland Being a Burden on Their Parents or Country, and for Making Them Beneficial to the Publick*. It is a satire in which the narrator recommends that Ireland's poor sell their children as food to the rich to escape poverty.

1731   Writes *Verses on the Death of Dr. Swift*, an obituary he wrote for himself (published in 1739).

1732   Publication of the poem "The Lady's Dressing Room."

Good friend and collaborator John Gay dies.

1735   Collected edition of Swift's *Works* published in Dublin;

Swift suffers from Ménière's Disease, resulting in periods of dizziness and nausea, and his memory is deteriorating.

Friend John Arbuthnot dies.

1736   Swift tells Pope, "I now neither read, nor write; nor remember, nor converse. All I have left is to walk, and ride."

1738   Swift slips into senility and begins to have violent outbursts.

1741   Guardians are appointed to take care of his affairs.

1742   Suffers a paralytic stroke.

1745   Swift dies on October 19. He is buried next to Esther Johnson, in accordance with his wishes. The bulk of his fortune funds a hospital for the mentally ill, which opens in 1757.

Swift wrote his own epitaph in Latin, a straight translation of which reads:

Here is laid the Body
of Jonathan Swift, Doctor of Sacred Theology,
Dean of this Cathedral Church,
where fierce Indignation
can no longer
injure the Heart.
Go forth, Voyager,
and copy, if you can,
this vigorous (to the best of his ability)
Champion of Liberty.